Coping with Behavioral Addictions

The Love Addiction Workbook

Information, Assessments, and Tools for Managing Life with a Behavioral Addiction

Ester R.A. Leutenberg and John J. Liptak, EdD

Whole Person Associates
Mental Health & Wellness Publishers
Duluth, Minnesota

Whole Person Associates

101 West 2nd Street, Suite 203
Duluth, MN 55802-5004

800-247-6789

Books@WholePerson.com
WholePerson.com

The Love Addiction Workbook

Printed in the United States of America

Editorial Director: Jack Kosmach
Art Director: Mathew Pawlak
Cover Design: Adam Sippola
Editor: Peg Johnson

Library of Congress Control Number: 2022942556
ISBN:978-1-57025-371-3

From the co-authors, Ester and John,
Our gratitude, thanks, and appreciation
to the following professionals:

Editorial Directors – Jack Kosmach and Peg Johnson

Editor and Lifelong Teacher – Eileen Regen, MEd, CIE

Reviewer – Niki Tilicki, MA Ed

Proofreader – Jay Leutenberg, CASA

Art Director – Mathew Pawlak

A Special Thank You
to
Whole Person Associates

for their interest in mental health issues.

Free PDF Download Available

To access your free PDF download of the assessment tools
and all of the reproducible activities in this workbook, go to:
https://WholePerson.com/store/TheLoveAddictionWorkbook2556.html

Understanding Behavioral Addictions

Many types of addictions exist. Addictions that have been talked about most have been substance abuse addictions. However, a behavioral addiction can take the same form as a physical dependence on a substance.

> ...it is the compulsive nature of the behavior that is often indicative of a behavioral addiction, or process addiction, in an individual. The compulsion to continually engage in an activity or behavior despite the negative impact on the person's ability to remain mentally and/or physically healthy and functional in the home and community defines behavioral addiction. The person may find the behavior rewarding psychologically or get a "high" while engaged in the activity, but may later feel guilt, remorse, or even overwhelmed by the consequences of that continued choice. Unfortunately, as is common for all who struggle with addiction, people living with behavioral addictions are unable to stop engaging in the behavior for any length of time without treatment and intervention.
>
> People are increasingly experiencing non-substance, behavioral addictions, and diminished control over their behavior. Behavioral addictions are no longer categorized as impulse disorders, and behavioral addictions are now viewed as true addictions, much like substance abuse.

~ American Addiction Centers (2019)

The National Institute of Health (2010) states:

> Growing evidence suggests that behavioral addictions resemble substance addictions in many domains, including natural history, phenomenology, tolerance, co-morbidity, overlapping genetic contribution, neurobiological mechanisms, and response to treatment.

The concept of addiction, for years adopted solely to indicate the use of psychotropic substances, is now being applied to describe a heterogeneous group of syndromes known as 'behavioral addictions,' 'no-drug addictions,' or 'new addictions.' Prevalence rates for such conditions, taken as a whole, are amongst the highest registered for mental disorders with social, cultural and economic implications. Individual forms of behavioral addictions are linked by a series of psychopathological features that include repetitive, persistent, and dysfunctional behaviors; loss of control over behavior despite the negative repercussions of the latter; compulsion to satisfy the need to implement the behavior; initial well-being produced by the behavior, craving, onset of tolerance, abstinence and, ultimately, a progressive, significant impairment of overall individual function.

Why Are They Called Behavioral Addictions?

Behavioral addictions constitute any maladaptive pattern of excessive behavior that manifests in physiological, psychological, and cognitive symptoms such as the following:

- **Continuance:** continuing the behavior despite knowing that this activity is creating or exacerbating physical, psychological, or interpersonal problems.

- **Intention effects:** inability to stick to one's routine, as evidenced by exceeding the amount of time devoted to the behavior or consistently going beyond the intended amount.

- **Lack of control:** unsuccessful attempts to reduce the level of the behavior or cease for a certain period of time.

- **Reduction in activities:** as a direct result of the behavior, social, familial, occupational, or recreational activities occur less often or are stopped.

- **Time:** a great deal of time is spent preparing for, engaging in, and recovering from the behavior.

- **Tolerance:** increasing the amount of the behavior to feel the desired effect, be it a buzz or a sense of accomplishment.

- **Withdrawal:** in the absence of the behavior, the person experiences adverse effects such as anxiety, irritability, restlessness, and sleep problems.

Addiction to Love

Love can be addictive when pursued for the wrong reasons. Love addiction is a compulsive, chronic craving and pursuit of romantic love to deal with emotional issues, gain a sense of security, and obtain self-worth from another person. During the infatuation stage, people addicted to love often believe they have security, only to be disappointed and feel empty again once the relationship intensity fades away, or they believe this is "the one," only to be disappointed once again. The negative consequences of an addiction to love can be severe, yet addicted people continue to believe that finding true love will make everything in life right. They feel that finding "the right person" will fix everything. It may! But often, it does not! Or it may for a while, but it does not last!

People addicted to love usually live in a chaotic world of desperate psychological need and emotional turmoil. They are afraid of being alone in life or rejected by others. They continually search for that special someone who will make them feel whole. They love to love! People addicted to love often have many intimate relationships. However, they are more attracted to the intense experience of "falling in love" than to the intimacy of a healthy relationship and making the most of these relationships. They often spend their lives hunting for "the one" who will make them whole. When engaged in this behavior, they do everything to prepare to meet someone, actually meet someone, and hope that the relationship will be fulfilling. Many of these behaviors revolve around meeting this "special" person. Love addicts spend much time and effort on the person to whom they are addicted. They often value this person above themselves, and their focus on the other person is often obsessive.

There is a significant difference between people seeking a healthy relationship and people addicted to love. The healthy "rush" of love can be the bond necessary to sustain an intimate relationship for individuals seeking a long-term relationship. People addicted to love are also addicted to the rush of first romance. However, they rarely allow relationships to develop beyond this initial, emotionally-intense state. When in a relationship, love addicts begin to feel disillusioned with their partner and feel detached, unhappy, restless, irritable, and discontent because the rush is gone, and they need to feel the rush again. These relationships can last a few days, quite a while, or many unhappy years. When they are not in a relationship, they feel desperate, unworthy, and alone until they find a new potential mate and experience the high of "falling in love" once again.

LOVE ADDICTION IN THE DSM-5

Although absent from the present diagnostic guidelines such as the World Health Organization 2018 International Classification of Diseases (ICD) and the Diagnostic and The American Psychiatric Association's 2018 Statistical Manual of Mental Disorders (DSM-5), experts have recognized that unhealthy relationships can quickly and easily become an addiction and lead to physical, occupational, social, and psychological problems.

Because of this danger to a person's well-being, look at the definition of substance dependence from the latest available edition of the Diagnostic and Statistical Manual of Mental Disorders from the American Psychological Association, the DSM-V: "When an individual persists in use of alcohol or other drugs despite problems related to use of the substance, substance dependence may be diagnosed." (American Psychiatric Association 2018.) As this quotation plainly states, the existence of "behavioral problems" is inherent in the definition of the disorder. In other words, it matters fundamentally whether harm, difficulty, or ill-consequences are associated with the reward-seeking behavior: the reward itself is not the problem, the behavior is the problem. An addiction theorist, Stanton Peele (quoted in Curley 2010), has suggested that the next edition of the DSM should include life-harming, compulsive involvement with sources of reward such as sex, food, and love in the category of addiction.

Unhealthy relationships and the rush from new love relationships can be a behavioral addiction that can be effectively treated using a range of cognitive and behavioral therapies.

Potential Signs of Love Addiction

Regardless of gender, love addicts spend much of their time either searching for the perfect love interest or disengaging from their current relationship so they can focus on a new one.

Signs of People Who Have a Love Addiction

They:
- Choose partners who are emotionally unavailable or abusive.
- Compulsively use sex and fantasy to fill the loneliness when they are not in a relationship.
- Constantly need and search for a romantic relationship.
- Determine that it is unbearable or emotionally difficult to be alone.
- Do not continue the relationship once the excitement has worn off.
- Fear the other person will break up the relationship.
- Feel desperate to please the other person.
- Feign interest in activities that aren't enjoyable to keep a partner or meet someone new.
- Find it difficult or impossible to leave unhealthy or abusive relationships despite repeated promises to loved ones.
- Give up meaningful friendships to please a romantic partner.
- Miss out on important family, career, or social experiences to search for a relationship.
- Mistake sexual experiences and new romantic excitement for love.
- Notice that they feel all alone when they are not in a relationship.
- Opt for partners who go against their values to keep or please a partner.
- Participate in activities that do not interest them.
- Pick partners who need a great deal of caretaking but do not try to meet their physical needs.
- Rely on romantic intensity to escape from stress and other emotional discomforts.
- Repeatedly return to previously painful relationships despite promises to oneself or others.
- Seek sexual or romantic passion to tolerate difficult experiences or emotions.
- Select partners who demand a great deal of attention but do not meet their own emotional needs.
- Use sex, seduction, guilt, and shame to "hook" or hold on to a partner.
- Utilize anonymous sex, porn, etc., to avoid "needing" someone, thereby avoiding all relationships.

Potential Origins

Much like people addicted to substances, love addicts search for something outside of themselves, such as a person, relationship, or experience that will fix their lives.

Examples of causes associated with a love addiction may include the following:

- Inadequate or inconsistent nurturing from parents as a child.
- Low levels of self-esteem.
- Absence of positive role models for committed relationships.
- Dependence on cultural images of perfect romantic love and "living happily ever after" endings.
- Lack of emotional stability.
- Lack of stability in life.
- Pattern of intensely stimulating romantic experiences to temporarily fix themselves and deal with emotional issues.
- Experiences from childhood: sexual assault, death of a parent, abuse, etc.

The Love Addiction Cycle

People who are addicted to love follow a set cycle with relationships. They engage in the following behaviors over and over again in search of the "perfect" person:

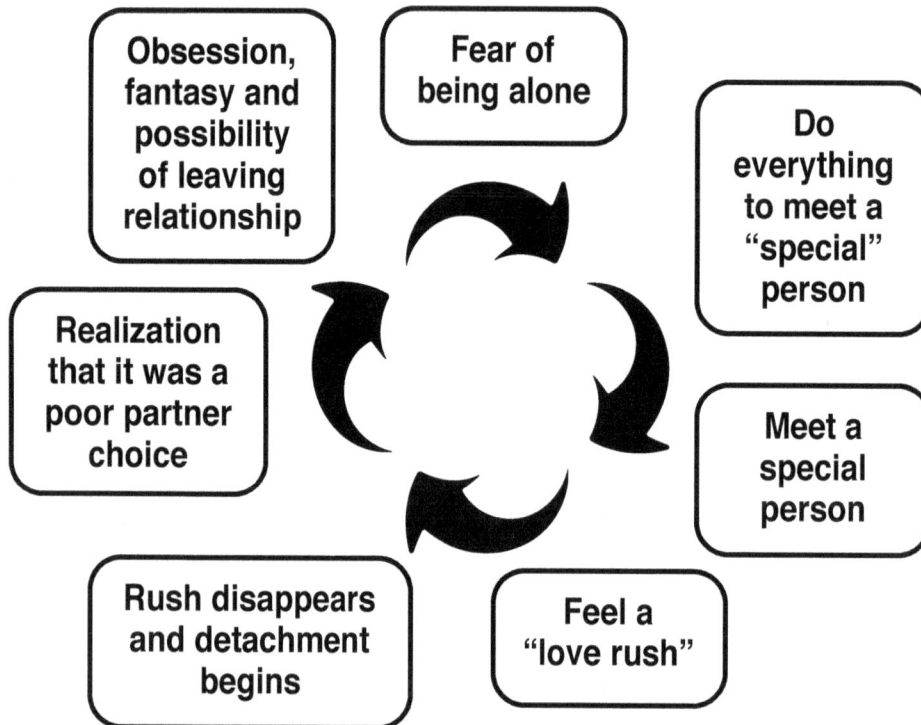

```
Obsession,              Fear of
fantasy and          being alone
possibility                              Do
of leaving                            everything
relationship                          to meet a
                                       "special"
                                        person

Realization
that it was a
poor partner                          Meet a
choice                                special
                                      person

   Rush disappears           Feel a
   and detachment          "love rush"
       begins
```

Relationship Addiction

A form of Love Addiction is a Relationship Addiction in which people are so afraid of being alone that they become addicted to any relationship, even an unhealthy one. The person addicted becomes codependent and will do anything to remain in the relationship. Module 3 of this workbook will address this love addiction problem.

Risk Factors

One must be aware of several unique risk factors when working with this population.

- A personal or family history of any other type of addiction.
- A family history of a psychological disorder such as depression, anxiety, or bipolar disorder.
- A history of unresolved trauma, neglect, abuse, abandonment, poor parenting, or domestic violence.
- A history of childhood sexual abuse.
- A history of childhood exposure to pornography, sexual situations, or other types of adult sexuality.

Many of these risk factors will be addressed in the activities, exercises, and assessments included in this workbook.

Using This Workbook

The purpose of *The Love Addiction Workbook* is to provide helping professionals with cognitive and behavioral assessments, tools, and exercises that can be utilized to treat the root psychological causes of a love addiction. It is designed to help people identify and change negative, unhealthy thoughts and behaviors that may have led to a love addiction. The activities contained in this workbook can help participants identify their triggers that can lead to an addiction to love and teach them ways to overcome and manage those triggers.

The Love Addiction Workbook **will help participants to achieve the following:**

- Understand recurring patterns that indicate a love addiction.
- Recognize that they are experiencing a love addiction problem.
- Reflect upon the behaviors that were part of and arose from the addiction.
- Build self-esteem and self-love so they are not so dependent on other people.
- Develop greater self-acceptance and the ability to change ineffective behaviors.
- Understand the triggers for preoccupation with finding the "perfect" person to make their life whole.
- Learn ways to live a new life without the need to obsess about finding a romantic partner to "fix" their life.

The Love Addiction Workbook is a practical tool for teachers, counselors, and helping professionals in their work with people suffering from behavioral addictions. Depending on the person's role using this workbook and the specific needs of the groups or individuals, the modules can be used individually or as part of an integrated curriculum. The facilitator may choose to administer one of the activities to a group or administer some of the assessments over one or more days as a workshop.

Confidentiality When Completing Activity Handouts

Participants will see the words NAME CODES [PJ1] on some of the activities in the modules. Instruct participants that when writing or speaking about anyone, they should use name codes for people to preserve privacy and anonymity. Using these codes will allow participants to explore their feelings without hurting anyone's feelings or fearing gossip, harm, or retribution. For example, a friend named Sherry, who **R**eads **M**any **B**ooks might be assigned a name code of **RMB** for a particular exercise. To protect others' identities, they will not use people's actual names or initials, just **NAME CODES**.

The Five Modules

This workbook contains five separate modules of activity-based handouts that will help participants learn more about themselves and their love addiction. These modules serve as avenues for self-reflection and group experiences revolving around topics of importance in the lives of the participants in the group.

The activities in this workbook are user-friendly and varied to provide a comprehensive way of analyzing, strengthening, and developing characteristics, skills, and attitudes for overcoming an addiction to love.

The activities and handouts in this workbook are reproducible. Minor revisions to suit client or group needs are permitted, but the copyright statement must be retained.

Module 1: Self-Esteem

This module will help participants become aware of and explore how their self-esteem is tied to their search for relationships to fill voids in their concept of self. Participants will understand the positive and negative self-evaluations they make and provide exercises for enhancing self-esteem.

Module 2: Fear of Being Alone

This module will help participants explore how their fear of being alone (autophobia) is affecting their lives and relationships. Often people who are addicted to love get involved in relationships because they are afraid of being alone. The activities in this module are designed to help participants overcome this fear.

Module 3: Codependency

This module will help participants examine codependency as a learned behavior based on an emotional and behavioral condition that affects an individual's ability to have a healthy, mutually satisfying relationship. They will examine this relationship addiction and how it keeps them in relationships that are one-sided, emotionally destructive, or abusive.

Module 4: Love Addiction Costs

This module will help participants realize the ways they are preoccupied, to the point of obsession with falling or being in love, and how they tend to behave in highly regrettable ways. They will learn tools and techniques to break the love addiction cycle.

Module 5: Love Yourself

This module will help participants discover ways they are so busy trying to find the perfect partner, or trying to stay in a relationship, that they do not take the time to accept themselves. They learn that to overcome an addiction to love, they must learn to have self-respect by understanding and loving who they truly are, their successes and mistakes and that they are worthy of love.

Different Types of Activity Handouts Included in This Workbook

A variety of materials are included in this reproducible workbook:

- **Action Plans** that assist participants in meeting the goals and objectives of treatment.

- **Assessments** that allow participants to explore their behavior. They can be used again to allow participants to track their progress.

- **Drawing and Doodling** to unleash the power of the right side of the brain.

- **Educational Pages** that provide insights and tips related to the topic.

- **Group Activities** to encourage collaboration among participants.

- **Journaling Activities** can help participants clarify their thoughts and feelings, thus gaining helpful self-knowledge.

- **Positive Affirmations** that allow participants to create formidable affirmations that they can post and repeat to themselves when impulses begin.

- **Quotation Pages** that allow participants to reflect on many powerful quotes and determine how they apply to their own lives.

- **Tables** that require participants to reflect on their lives in the past, understand themselves in the present, and react more effectively in the future.

References

American Addiction Centers (2019). Behavioral Addictions. https://americanaddictioncenters.org/behavioral-addictions

American Psychiatric Association (2018). Diagnostic and Statistical Manual of Mental Disorders (DSM–5), https://www.psychiatry.org/psychiatrists/practice/dsm

Curley B. DSM-V: major changes to addictive disease classifications. Recovery today online. 2010 Accessed at: http://www.recoverytoday.net/articles/143-dsm-v-major-changes-to-addictive-disease-classifications/

National Institute of Health (2010). Introduction to Behavioral Addictions. https://www.ncbi.nlm.nih.gov/pmc/articles/PMC3164585

World Health Organization (2018). International Classification of Diseases (ICD) Information Sheet. https://www.who.int/classifications/icd/factsheet/en/

Table of Contents

(Continued on page xiii)

Table of Contents

(Continued on page xiv)

Table of Contents

Self-Esteem

Name _____

Date _____

Self-Esteem Assessment
Introduction and Directions

People addicted to love usually have relatively low self-esteem and look for relationships to fill voids in their concept of self. In general, self-esteem is what you think about yourself. Self-esteem includes both the positive and negative self-evaluations you make. People with superior self-esteem have a realistic, positive self-concept. It reflects self-respect and a feeling of worth that's not determined by comparison to others. People with positive self-esteem also do not feel the need for approval from others.

The Self-Esteem Assessment contains 20 statements related to one's self-esteem. It can help you explore how you view yourself. Read each one and decide whether it describes you. If the statement describes you, circle the number in the YES column next to that item. If the statement does not describe you, circle the number in the NO column next to that item.

In the following example, the circled two indicates that the person completing this assessment believes that the statement is true for them:

	YES	NO
When I am alone and not in a relationship:		
I compare myself to others in a negative way	(2)	1

This is not a test. Since there are no right or wrong answers, do not spend too much time thinking about your answers. Be sure to respond to every statement.

BE HONEST!

If you choose, no one else needs to see the results.

(Turn to the next page and begin.)

Self-Esteem Assessment

Name _____ Date _____

This will only be accurate if you respond honestly. No one else needs to see this if you choose.

	YES	NO
When I am alone and not in a relationship:		
I compare myself to others in a negative way	2	1
I find fault with myself	2	1
I beat myself up with "I shoulda" statements	2	1
I project self-criticism onto others and imagine they judge me	2	1
I do not try new things because I may fail	2	1
I feel bad about myself	2	1
I doubt my instincts and decisions about relationships	2	1
I ignore my needs and wants	2	1
I do not set boundaries around abuse, criticism, or exploitation	2	1
I refuse to forgive myself for my relationship choices	2	1
I avoid social situations	2	1
I have feelings of inadequacy	2	1
I cannot accept compliments	2	1
I neglect my own needs, particularly emotional ones	2	1
I put the needs of others ahead of my own	2	1
I have low expectations	2	1
I cannot maintain a relationship when I finally have one	2	1
I seek relationships to fill a void in my life	2	1
I cannot trust my own judgment of people	2	1
I don't like myself	2	1

Self-Esteem TOTAL = _____

Go to the next page for scoring assessment results,
profile interpretation, and individual description.

Self-Esteem Assessment

Descriptions and Profile Interpretations

The assessment you just completed is designed to measure your self-esteem. The Yes items are indicative of low self-esteem. For each item on the previous page, count the scores you circled. Put that total on the line marked TOTAL at the end of the assessment.   Then, transfer your total to this space below::

Self-Esteem TOTAL   =   _____

Assessment Profile Interpretation

By circling even ONE Yes answer, you could be at risk of having relationship problems. The more Yes answers you circled, the greater your risk of having an addiction to love and unhealthy relationships.

The HIGHER your score on the Self-Esteem Assessment, the more of an issue you probably have with your self-esteem in relationships, and the more likely you are to experience an addiction to love. Place on X on the line below for your score.

Self-Esteem (How you feel about yourself – your self-concept)

20 = Low	30 = Moderate	40 = High

Begin by making copies of this reminder below and post them in various visible places.

Self-Esteem, Self-Love, Self-Respect, and Self-Worth.
There is a reason why these all start with the word <u>Self</u>!
You cannot find them in anyone else!
You can work on them and find them in your <u>Self</u>!

Nobody is Perfect

Many people have certain expectations and are perfectionistic. In each hexagon, write a quality that you seek in a partner. Next to each quality, explain whether this is a realistic expectation or not, and why.

Examples: kind, fun, sexy, rich, empathetic, trustworthy, ambitious, independent, mature, etc.

My Perfect Partner

© 2023 WHOLE PERSON ASSOCIATES, 101 WEST 2ND STREET, SUITE 203, DULUTH MN 55802 • 800-247-6789 • WHOLEPERSON.COM

Activities I Relished

Many people who are addicted to love spend so much of their time looking for the "perfect" partner that they give up many activities they loved in the past (writing, singing, camping, baking, etc.). To feel better about yourself and not have all of your self-esteem tied up in your search for the perfect partner, you need to think about and start engaging in activities that you relished in the past.

In the four spaces below, write about, draw, or doodle some of those activities.

1	2

3	4

Circle one you will agree to participate in within the next week. 1 2 3 4

Comparisons

Many people who are addicted to love fall into the comparison habit. They compare themselves and their lives to other people in their life, or people on television or in the newspaper. This can be a destructive way of looking at who you really are and what you want in life. There will always be someone who has it better than you or SEEMS to have it better than you. You need to replace this habit!

Read the following quote, and answer the questions that follow it.

Comparison is painful. Don't be cowed by other people's pretty pictures. When you feel unimpressive or irrelevant, that has nothing to do with what you're actually capable of.
~ Jennifer Egan

To whom do you compare yourself? (USE NAME CODES)

_____

_____

_____

How is the above comparison painful to you?

_____

_____

_____

What is it about this "pretty picture" that allows you to feel like you have less or you are inferior?

_____

_____

_____

How do you feel about yourself from this comparison?

_____

_____

_____

What do you have that is as good or better in comparison?

_____

_____

_____

Things I Feel Good About

If you are addicted to love, you might not feel good about yourself, and it probably shows in your need for a relationship to fill the void of low self-esteem. You have many things to feel good about, and there are many activities you can engage in or people you can be with to feel good about yourself.

List some of the activities that will help you feel more positive about yourself.

1.

I feel positive about myself when I am _____

I will engage in this activity by: _____

_____

_____

2.

I feel positive about myself when I am _____

I will engage in this activity by: _____

_____

_____

3.

I feel positive about myself when I am _____

I will engage in this activity by: _____

_____

_____

4.

I feel positive about myself when I am _____

I will engage in this activity by: _____

_____

_____

5.

I feel positive about myself when I am _____

I will engage in this activity by: _____

_____

_____

Choose and circle one of the above activities that you will start first?   1   2   3   4   5

When? _____

With Whom? _____

Realistic Thoughts

Just what is negative self-talk? It is the negative inner dialog that goes on in your head.

If you are addicted to love and have had many different relationships that have not worked out well, you probably engage in constant negative self-talk about yourself and the objects of your affection.

Below, identify some of your negative self-talks, consider the validity of them, and replace them with more realistic thoughts.

Negative Self-Talk	Valid or Not Valid?	More Realistic Talk
Example: I will never find a fulfilling relationship.	*Not valid. I have had some okay relationships before.*	*I will probably find a partner again, but I will need to figure out what I can do to help us have a positive outcome.*

Ways to have more realistic thoughts and to monitor your internal, negative thinking:

- Catch Your Inner Critic: Learn to notice when you're being self-critical so you can quickly stop the thoughts.
- Remember That Thoughts Are Not Always Realistic: Thinking negative things about yourself may seem accurate, but they often are not.
- Replace the Bad with Some Good: One of the best ways to combat negative self-talk is by replacing it with more positive thoughts.

A Challenge and Goals

People who do not have a partner and are addicted to love have goals that usually revolve around searching for and finding the perfect partner. It is helpful to set other non-love-related goals or challenges to pursue. When you put yourself out there, you never know who you might meet, how you will meet, and what captivating new ideas that meeting might uncover. For example, you might work on a college degree, find a better job, start a business, learn a foreign language, join a choir or band, write a book, exercise, volunteer at a soup kitchen, etc.

Set yourself a challenge and identify some goals to achieve the challenge.
Make sure it is a realistic one!

The challenge: _____

_____

_____

_____

Realistic long-term goal: _____

_____

_____

_____

Realistic short-term goals: _____

_____

_____

_____

How I will meet the goals and achieve the challenge: _____

_____

_____

_____

Put Your Self-Care on the Calendar

People addicted to love are usually looking for other people to make them feel whole. Rather than looking to others to fill voids in your life, look at ways to fill some of those voids yourself.

Block out time for some type of self-care every day on a calendar. *(Ex: exercise, pamper yourself, hobby time, spa, hot tub, massage, walk in the park, spend time with family, go to the movie and get popcorn, etc.)*

In the spaces on this weekly calendar below, list how you will take care of yourself every day.

Day	My Self-Care	How It Can Help Me
Monday		
Tuesday		
Wednesday		
Thursday		
Friday		
Saturday		
Sunday		

Self-Care Things to Remember:
- This self-care time is non-negotiable. If a potential conflict arises, say that you are not available. This time must take precedence over anything but an emergency.
- If you must make a change, reschedule your self-care time for another day that week.

© 2023 WHOLE PERSON ASSOCIATES, 101 WEST 2ND STREET, SUITE 203, DULUTH MN 55802 • 800-247-6789 • WHOLEPERSON.COM

I AM Good Enough

People addicted to love feel like they must have significant people in their lives to feel good about themselves. Think about it. You have a lot to feel grateful for; you are accomplished; you have done good things; you have helped; you care about others, etc.

DIG DEEP, do not be modest and identify some of your accomplishments.

I Am Grateful For	I Have Accomplished a Lot	I Do, and Have Done, Good Things
My very special family.	I earned a degree in art and have a great job at a studio.	I take care of my parents, who are elderly.

Sometimes good enough is good enough.
~ Julie Bowen

Enjoy and Enhance Self-Esteem

Many people are searching for something missing in themselves that appeals to others. They search for the perfect partner, only to be disappointed. A better way to approach relationships is to work on what you feel is missing in you that keeps you from being involved in a healthy relationship.

You need to begin engaging in activities that you enjoy and make you feel good about yourself.

Identify activities that you admire in others and want to try. This might make a difference in your life!

Activities I Enjoy/Might Enjoy	Why I Enjoy It/Might Enjoy It	How It Enhances/Might Enhance My Self-Esteem
Example: Playing chess against a computer.	*It is very calculated, and you need to train yourself to look for patters.*	*If I practice, I will master this difficult skill, and that will make me feel good about myself.*

Negative or Positive

Many people who are addicted to love wind up being negative because of relationships that have not been successful. Then, they attract friends who have the same attitude and feed into the participants' negativity and frustrations. This then feeds the need to search for a partner to love.

You need to spend less time with these negative people and build friendships with more positive, supportive people who value you.

Identify the positive people in your life. (USE NAME CODES)

Positive People	Why They Are <u>Good</u> for Me	How I Can Spend <u>More</u> Time With Them

Identify the people in your life that affect you in a negative way. (USE NAME CODES)

Negative People	Why They Are <u>Not Good</u> for Me	How I Can Spend <u>Less</u> Time With Them

I Have Achievements

Think about all the things you've accomplished. In each circle, write something you have accomplished or done that makes you feel proud.

Acknowledge your achievements, no matter how small. If you have more than six, write them on the sides. Post this paper somewhere that you can easily see it to review it when you need a reminder of your ability to get things done and do them well.

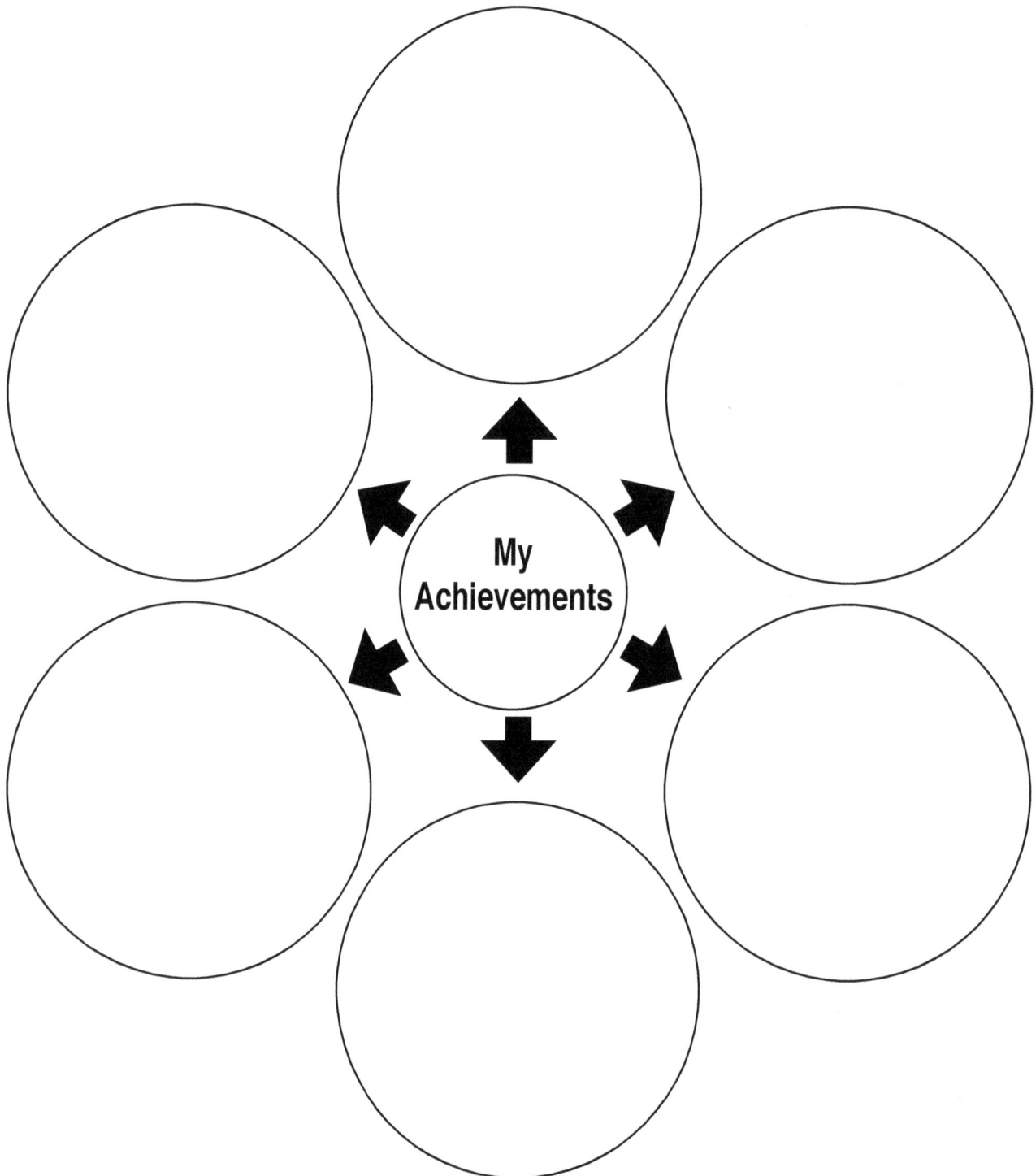

My Achievements

What Does Success Mean to You?

People addicted to love can only imagine success if they have a great partner-relationship with someone. However, one can have success in many other areas of life.

Areas of My Life	Success with a Non-Partner	Ways I Will Achieve It	How Do I Feel?
Example: Family	*A better relationship with my brother.*	*Visit him more, and take an interest in his life.*	*It makes me feel good, and it sure makes him feel good too!*
Family			
Friends			
Work			
Spare Time			
Personal Wellness			
Self-Care			
Other			

Success comes from knowing that you did your best to become the
best that you are capable of becoming.
~ John Wooden

Tame Your Inner Critic

Inner Critic: An inner voice that judges criticizes, or demeans a person
whether or not the self-criticism is objectively justified.

People are often their own worst critics. A highly active inner critic can drag down one's emotional well-being and self-esteem.

Your inner voice whispers destructive thoughts in your mind. For example:
- *"You're fat."*
- *"You're unlovable."*
- *"You're inadequate."*

A good place to start with raising your self-esteem is by learning how to identify and replace the voice of your own inner critic.

List one of your inner critic thoughts. _____

_____

_____

Identify what your critical inner voice is telling you. _____

_____

_____

Why is this thought unrealistic? _____

_____

_____

Replace this unrealistic thought with a more realistic thought. _____

_____

_____

Your inner critic is simply a part of you that needs more self-love.
~ Amy Leigh Mercree

I Need a Relationship

People with a love addiction often need a relationship to feel whole. They do not feel good about themselves unless they are in a relationship. They need someone to fill a void.

Complete the sentence fragments by journaling your thoughts.

I need a relationship or I...

_____

_____

_____

If I'm not in a relationship, I find myself...

_____

_____

_____

When not in a relationship, I feel as if I...

_____

_____

_____

When I'm not in a relationship, I wish I could...

_____

_____

_____

When I'm not in a relationship, I don't want to...

_____

_____

_____

When I'm in a relationship, I feel...

_____

_____

_____

Self-Appreciation

Self-appreciation is about not blaming yourself for making mistakes and forgiving yourself when you do. Self-appreciation is about saying "thank you" to yourself for all the things you have done but have taken for granted.

Self-appreciation is a habit that must be developed. Take a deep breath, slow down and ask yourself this question: What are some things I can appreciate about myself?

On the top line, list three things you appreciate about yourself. Then in the space below, list some of the reasons why each is important to you.

Example:

3 THINGS I APPRECIATE ABOUT MYSELF		
I appreciate my creativity	I appreciate my friendly nature.	I appreciate my work ethic
I want to begin engaging in more creative activities when I feel lonely.	I want to join a scrapbooking club to meet other people with interests like me.	I want to be a great employee and concentrate on getting promoted.

Now you try!

3 THINGS I APPRECIATE ABOUT MYSELF		

© 2023 WHOLE PERSON ASSOCIATES, 101 WEST 2ND STREET, SUITE 203, DULUTH MN 55802 • 800-247-6789 • WHOLEPERSON.COM

Quotes about Self-Esteem

On the lines that follow the four quotes below,
describe which quote(s) speak to you and your self-esteem

Think like a queen. A queen is not afraid to fail.
Failure is another stepping stone to greatness.
~ Oprah

To love oneself is the beginning of a lifelong romance.
~ Oscar Wilde

You yourself, as much as anybody in the entire universe,
deserve your love and affection.
~ Sharon Salzberg

Wanting to be someone else is a waste of the person you are.
~ Marilyn Monroe

Which quote especially speaks to you about self-esteem? Why?

_____

_____

_____

_____

_____

_____

_____

_____

_____

_____

_____

_____

_____

Love

Fear of Being Alone

Name _____

Date _____

Fear of Being Alone Assessment
Introduction and Directions

Autophobia is the fear of being alone or lonely. Being alone or lonely, even in a usually comforting place like home, can result in severe anxiety for people with this condition.

Many people who are addicted to love experience autophobia and feel they need another person or other people around to feel safe. It is important to explore how you feel when you are alone and whether your fear of being alone pushes you into unhealthy relationship after unhealthy relationship.

The following assessment contains 20 statements that describe fears about being alone and not being in a relationship. Read each of the them and decide whether or not it describes you. If the statement describes you, place a checkmark in the box in front of it. If the statement does not describe you, leave the box in front of the statement empty.

In the following example, the first statement is descriptive of the person completing the assessment, but the second is not:

When I am not in a relationship:

☑ I feel alone and lonely.

□ I am terrified of being alone.

This is not a test. Since there are no right or wrong answers, do not spend too much time thinking about your answers. Be sure to respond to every statement.

BE HONEST!

If you choose, no one else needs to see the results.

(Turn to the next page and begin.)

Fear of Being Alone Assessment

Name _____ Date _____

This will only be accurate if you respond honestly. No one else needs to see this if you choose.

When I am not in a relationship:

☐ I feel alone and lonely.

☐ I am terrified of being alone.

☐ I fantasize to overcome the feeling of loneliness.

☐ I am afraid of being abandoned.

☐ I find it emotionally difficult to be alone.

☐ I seek the rush of first romance, not long-lasting love.

☐ I crave and search for romantic relationships.

☐ I will do anything to avoid feeling vulnerable.

☐ I will have sex with anyone to overcome my feeling of loneliness.

☐ I feel desperate to find someone when I feel alone.

☐ I desperately need to find the perfect person for me.

☐ I fear approaching someone new and being rejected.

☐ I believe that my soul mate is out there, somewhere.

☐ I find life to be unbearable when I do not have a partner.

☐ I use anonymous sex or compulsive masturbation to avoid needing someone.

☐ I miss out on family or social experiences to search for a romantic relationship.

☐ I frantically search for a partner to tolerate my difficult experiences or emotions.

☐ I do not attend important career events because I am searching for a relationship.

☐ I am addicted to the adrenaline rush of meeting and getting to know someone new.

☐ I engage in sex, seduction, and manipulation—anything to try to hook a partner.

TOTAL Checked Responses = _____

Go to the next page for scoring assessment
results, profile interpretation, and individual descriptions

Fear of Being Alone Assessment

Scoring and Profile Interpretations

The *Fear of Being Alone Assessment* you just completed is designed to measure your fear of not being in a relationship. **Count the number of items you checked on the assessment.**

Put that total on the line marked TOTAL on the assessment at the bottom of the page. Then, transfer your total to this space below:

TOTAL Checked Answers   =   _____

Assessment Profile Interpretation

Put an X on the continuum line below, indicating the number of items you checked on the assessment.

The HIGHER your score on the Fear of Being Alone Assessment, the more addiction you are experiencing.

0 = Low	10 = Moderate	20 = High

By checking even ONE statement, you could be experiencing issues in your life that may be due to an addiction to love. The more items you checked, the greater the risk you will experience the many issues of an addiction to love, now and in the future.

Is your score valid? Were you honest when completing the assessment?

_____

_____

What is your reaction to your score?

_____

_____

Do you feel you need or want to do something about your love and relationship issues?

_____

_____

When I Am Alone, I ...

Loneliness can be emotionally painful, and it can push people to seek the buzz from being in love.

On this page, focus on how you feel when you are lonely. Complete the following sentence starters to explore your feelings related to your fears of being alone.

When I am alone, I...

_____

_____

_____

When I am alone, I...

_____

_____

_____

When I am alone, I...

_____

_____

_____

When I am alone, I...

_____

_____

_____

> Loneliness is such an omnipotent and painful threat to many persons
> that they have little conception of the positive values of solitude and even,
> at times, are frightened at the prospect of being alone.
> **~ Rollo May**

Pressure to Find a Partner

People addicted to love feel an internal pressure to meet and develop a relationship with someone who will make them happy and fix the problem of being alone. There is also pressure from peers, family, and society in general, to find a partner or to be in a stable, long-term relationship.

Below, identify the people (including yourself) who pressure you to find a partner.

The Pressure I Feel	The Pressure Comes From ... (USE NAME CODES)	Ways This Affects Me and My Behavior
Example: To be in a permanent relationship.	*LKA*	*I spend all of my time thinking about finding someone rather than focusing on my career.*

I want to wake up every day and do whatever comes in my mind,
and not feel pressure or obligations to do anything else in my life.
~ Michael Jordan

Just Settling

People addicted to love often settle for someone who is not a suitable partner. When this occurs, they feel stuck in the relationship, and often they are not assertive enough to leave it. They wind up being involved with an unsuitable partner because they fear being alone or lonely.

Below, describe some of the relationships you have had with unsuitable partners, and define what you learned from the relationship.

Unsuitable Relationship (USE NAME CODES)	What Occurred?	What I Learned
FLP	She was verbally abusive, and at times she would get physical. I was afraid to leave her.	I am okay on my own and do not need to stay in scary relationships.
MBB	We had absolutely nothing in common other than sex. I couldn't have a conversation with him without our getting into an argument and not talking for days.	I need to be able to talk about politics, my job, or what to have for dinner without worrying that anything I would say would create a huge problem.

Some things to remember:
You will not be able to change your partner's behavior.
You can change your expectations and responses.
You need to replace old thoughts with new affirmations.
You need to be assertive in your relationships.

© 2023 WHOLE PERSON ASSOCIATES, 101 WEST 2ND STREET, SUITE 203, DULUTH MN 55802 • 800-247-6789 • WHOLEPERSON.COM

Ways People Have Treated Me

People addicted to love will often accept and put up with inappropriate behavior in relationships just to avoid being by themselves and being lonely.

In the squares below, list ways you have been treated poorly in relationships. In the space next to that square, list the fear you experienced that kept you accepting the inappropriate behavior.

Ways I Have Been Treated Poorly

I Am Afraid To Be Alone

Under each characteristic of autophobia, place an X on the line to show how much or how little the statement describes you. On the dotted line below each characteristic, write why you rated yourself that way.

BE HONEST!

I am afraid to be alone.

_____

0 (Not Much)   5 (Somewhat)   10 (Very Much)

I would rather be in an unhealthy relationship than no relationship at all.

_____

0 (Not Much)   5 (Somewhat)   10 (Very Much)

I get panicky thinking about being alone.

_____

0 (Not Much)   5 (Somewhat)   10 (Very Much)

I constantly search for a partner so I will not be lonely.

_____

0 (Not Much)   5 (Somewhat)   10 (Very Much)

I am so afraid of being alone that it is all I think about .

_____

0 (Not Much)   5 (Somewhat)   10 (Very Much)

My fear of being alone affects my self-esteem, work, friendships, etc.

_____

0 (Not Much)   5 (Somewhat)   10 (Very Much)

HIGHER SCORES (Very Much) on each statement indicates that you are experiencing signs of autophobia. You need to be sure that this fear is not prompting an addiction to love.

MEDIUM SCORES (Somewhat) indicate that you are experiencing some signs of autophobia.

LOWER SCORES (Not Much) indicate that you are not experiencing many signs of autophobia.

© 2023 WHOLE PERSON ASSOCIATES, 101 WEST 2ND STREET, SUITE 203, DULUTH MN 55802 • 800-247-6789 • WHOLEPERSON.COM

The Right Person

People addicted to love often believe that a partner in a romantic relationship will make them feel valuable, alive, worthy, and admirable. For each of the sentence fragments, write a short story that describes how you feel.

If I find the right person, I will be more valuable because... _____

_____

_____

If I find the right person, I will be more alive because... _____

_____

_____

If I find the right person, I will be more admirable because... _____

_____

_____

If I find the right person, I will... _____

_____

_____

If I find the right person, I will be whole because... _____

_____

_____

If I don't find the right person, I will still be okay because... _____

_____

_____

I Can't Change (Part 1)

People addicted to love often do not change the cycle of searching for the perfect partner, getting involved, becoming disillusioned, and then starting the search again.

Following are some of the thoughts that you might have about love and relationships. Place a checkmark by the ones that apply to you, then write about how the statement is true in your life.

☐ I have few healthy boundaries. I become sexually involved or emotionally attached to people without knowing them.

_____

_____

_____

☐ Because I fear abandonment and loneliness, I stay with and return to painful, destructive relationships.

_____

_____

_____

☐ I conceal my dependency needs from myself and others, and I grow more isolated and alienated from friends and loved ones.

_____

_____

_____

☐ Because I fear emotional and/or sexual deprivation, I compulsively pursue and involve myself in one relationship after another.

_____

_____

_____

☐ I confuse love with neediness.

_____

_____

_____

☐ I feel empty and incomplete when I am alone.

_____

_____

_____

☐ I confuse love with pity.

_____

_____

_____

I Can't Change (Part 2)

People addicted to love often feel they can't change the cycle of searching for the perfect partner, getting involved, becoming disillusioned in the relationship, and then starting the search again.

Following are some of the thoughts that you might have about love and relationships. Place a checkmark by the ones that apply to you, then write about how the statement is true in your life.

☐ Even though I fear intimacy and commitment, I continually search for relationships and sexual contacts.

_____
_____
_____

☐ I use sex or emotional dependence as substitutes for nurturing care and support.

_____
_____
_____

☐ I become immobilized or seriously distracted by romantic or sexual obsessions or fantasies.

_____
_____
_____

☐ I avoid taking responsibility for myself by attaching myself to people who are emotionally unavailable.

_____
_____
_____

☐ I stay bound to emotional dependency, romantic intrigue, or compulsive sexual activities.

_____
_____
_____

☐ I assign magical qualities to other people.

_____
_____
_____

☐ I idealize and pursue romantic partners, then blame them for not fulfilling my fantasies and expectations.

_____
_____
_____

Brief, but Intense Relationships

People addicted to love tend to become involved in brief, intense romantic relationships. If they are involved in a long-term relationship, it is usually characterized by many highs and lows. In some cases, love addicts completely withdraw from and leave these romantic or sexual relationships to avoid feelings of vulnerability, or the other person does the same.

Complete the table below.

Relationship (USE NAME CODES)	Length of Relationship	Who Withdrew?	Why?
NHO	Three months	Me	He was not as perfect as I needed him to be, and the buzz of the relationship wore off.
GFJ	One and half years	She	I wanted her to be with me all the time and did not want her to see any of her friends. She felt I was too needy.

Romantic love is an addiction.
~ Helen Fisher

Agree? ☐ or Disagree? ☐ Why? _____

Numbing Out

People addicted to love usually learn early in life that an effective way to numb out and not feel difficult emotions (shame, fear, depression, guilt, anger, and anxiety) is to escape into the intense and distracting chemical rush of romantic fantasy. For example, a person addicted to love will focus on the new partner and how wonderful their life will be together and can avoid focusing on difficult issues and the emotions that go with those situations. In this respect, love with a new partner is a way to escape the real world.

What difficult emotions or situations do you numb out by searching for a new relationship?

List a time when you numbed out. _____
_____
_____

What emotion, or life situation, were you numbing out and escaping from? _____
_____
_____

How did you go about searching for a new loving relationship? _____
_____
_____

How did this search help you to numb out? _____
_____
_____

Describe this relationship. _____
_____
_____

How else could you have handled this situation? _____
_____
_____

What did you learn from this process? _____
_____
_____

Face Your Fear

Many people who continually search for the perfect partner fear being alone. They do not feel complete unless they are in a romantic, loving situation. They usually search for others to make up for their inadequacies.

To face your fear, try making a collection of advantages and disadvantages of spending time alone versus constantly searching for others. Draw, doodle, make a cartoon or write about disadvantages and advantages.

Disadvantages of Being Alone	Advantages of Being Alone

I'm a big believer in living out your dreams and facing your fears.
~ Brock Lesnar

© 2023 WHOLE PERSON ASSOCIATES, 101 WEST 2ND STREET, SUITE 203, DULUTH MN 55802 • 800-247-6789 • WHOLEPERSON.COM

The Cost of My Fears

Your fears of being alone and your constant search for the perfect partner can have a tremendous cost for the rest of your life. It is important to consider the costs:

- Your relationships *(I have not socialized with friends for a while).*
- Your passions *(I haven't skied because I'm on the lookout for a new love to ski with).*
- Your self-development *(I have wanted to learn Spanish for a long time, etc.).*

Below, list your fears and what they cost you.

Where I Am Afraid	Fear	The Cost of My Fear
My Friendships		
My Health		
My Non-Love Passions		
My Relationships		
My Self-Development		
My Spirituality		
My Work/Career		

Relationship Fantasies

Many people who are addicted to love believe that life should have a fantasy ending. While these endings are prevalent in popular culture, they do not always occur in real life. To appreciate happiness, we need to have some sadness. People addicted to love are often preoccupied with the notions of love and relationships as expressed in music, movies, television shows, and books.

Below, list the source and describe some of the "happily ever after" relationships you fantasize about below.

Name of Movie, TV show, Music, or Fiction	How I Fantasize About It	How It Affects My Relationships
TV show "How I Met Your Mother."	I like the main character, Ted. I always feel like the perfect person like him is just around the corner for me!	I keep looking for the same perfection as Ted, and after a while, I realize my guy is just not the same as Ted!

The good ended happily, and the bad unhappily. That is what fiction means.
~ Oscar Wilde

Do you agree with this quotation from Oscar Wilde about movies, TV, books, music lyrics, etc.?

Picture Your Fears

People addicted to love often stay in permanent, unhealthy relationships because of their fears. They fear the prospect of being alone, being abandoned, and being rejected by potential partners.

Below, draw what each of these fears looks like.

What does your fear of being alone look like?

What does your fear of being abandoned look like?

What does your fear of being rejected look like?

My Internal Void

If one is addicted to love, one may have an internal void that just cannot be filled in solitude or without a romantic relationship. This void can be seen in the form of thoughts: I don't matter, I am unworthy, I am emotionally empty, I am unlovable, I don't deserve love.

In the graphic below, write about your thoughts that are fueled by your internal void.

My Internal Void

© 2023 WHOLE PERSON ASSOCIATES, 101 WEST 2ND STREET, SUITE 203, DULUTH MN 55802 • 800-247-6789 • WHOLEPERSON.COM

Quotes about the Fear of Being Alone

Read all three of the quotations below.

#1
Being alone and actually sitting with our own thoughts can lead to such growth and realizations that are rare in our everyday busy lives.
~ Kourtney Kardashian

#2
I have learned over the years that when one's mind is made up, this diminishes fear; knowing what must be done does away with fear.
~ Rosa Parks

#3

On a personal level, change is a hard thing for me.
~ Chyler Leigh

Pick a quote that sounds like you and explain why. #_____

_____

_____

_____

Pick one that inspires you to do better and explain how you will do that. # _____

_____

_____

_____

Pick a quote that taught you something and explain what it taught you. # _____

_____

_____

_____

Write your own quote regarding relationships and what you have learned.

_____

_____

_____

Love

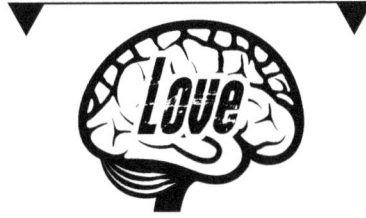

Codependency

Name _____

Date _____

Codependency Assessment
Introduction and Directions

Codependency is a learned behavior. It is based on an emotional and behavioral condition that affects an individual's ability to have a healthy, mutually satisfying relationship.

Codependency is also known as "relationship addiction" because people with codependency often form or maintain relationships that are one-sided, emotionally destructive, and abusive.

People with an addiction to love are often drawn into codependent relationships because of their fear of being alone. To them, a codependent relationship is better than being alone.

The following assessment contains 20 statements that describe some of the characteristics of a codependent relationship. Read each of the statements and decide if the statement describes you. If it does, place a checkmark in the box in front of the statement. If the statement does not describe you, leave the box in front of the statement empty.

In the following example, the first statement is descriptive of the person completing the assessment, but the second is not:

When in a relationship:

☑ I am desperate to please my partner.

☐ I am fearful of my partner's unhappiness.

As we've reminded you before, this is not a test. Since there are no right or wrong answers, do not spend too much time thinking about your answers. Be sure to respond to every statement.

BE HONEST!

If you choose, no one else needs to see the results.

(Turn to the next page and begin.)

Codependency Assessment

Name _____ Date _____

This will only be accurate if you respond honestly. No one else needs to see this if you choose.

When in a relationship:

☐ I am desperate to please my partner.

☐ I am fearful of my partner's unhappiness.

☐ I mistake intense sexual experiences for true love.

☐ I mistake new romantic excitement for true love.

☐ I cannot maintain a relationship once the newness wears off.

☐ I choose partners who are emotionally unavailable.

☐ I often feel that I am verbally or physically abused.

☐ I seem to choose partners who demand a great deal of attention and caretaking.

☐ I am often with a partner who does not meet, or even try to meet, my needs.

☐ I engage in activities that don't interest me to please my partner.

☐ I have given up important interests and friendships to please my partner.

☐ I cannot leave unhealthy relationships despite my repeated determination to do so.

☐ I often return to previously painful relationships.

☐ I always become obsessed with my partner.

☐ I lie to or manipulate my partner.

☐ I control my partners or convince them to stay in the relationship.

☐ I do what it takes to please the person.

☐ I have unrealistic expectations of the person.

☐ I smother the person.

☐ I act as a caretaker.

TOTAL Checked Responses = _____

Go to the next page for scoring assessment
results, profile interpretation, and individual descriptions

Codependency Assessment

Scoring and Profile Interpretations

The assessment you just completed is designed to measure your codependency in your relationships.

Count the number of items you checked on the Codependency Assessment. Put that total on the line marked TOTAL on the assessment at the bottom of the page. Then transfer your total to the space below:

TOTAL Checked Answers   =   _____

Assessment Profile Interpretation

By checking even ONE statement, you could be experiencing problems in your life due to a codependent relationship. The more items you checked, the greater the risk you have for experiencing many negative issues in your relationships.

The HIGHER your score on the Codependency Assessment, the more of a love addiction you are experiencing. Mark your score on the scale below.

0 = Low	**10 = Moderate**	**20 = High**

By checking even ONE statement, you could be experiencing issues in your life that may be due to an addiction to love. The more items you checked, the greater the risk you will experience the many issues of an addiction to love, now and in the future.

How honest were you when you completed the assessment? Is your score valid?

_____

_____

What is your reaction to your score?

_____

_____

What do you feel you need to do about your codependency issues?

_____

_____

Boundary Impairment

Boundaries are limits you set so that others do not take advantage of you. These limits defend your personal dignity and self-concept. Boundaries are psychological and emotional lines that people in a relationship should not cross. These boundaries are psychological limits that mark the distinction between behavior that does not cause emotional harm and behavior that does cause emotional harm. People addicted to love usually enter relationships with undisclosed boundaries.

Examples of boundaries relayed from one partner to the other:
- *Will not disclose too much information in the initial stages of meeting someone.*
- *Will not tolerate unhealthy behaviors from their partner.*
- *Will not be responsible for the other's feelings.*
- *Will not be upset if the other person says NO.*
- *Will not display extreme neediness.*
- *Will not make unrealistic demands.*
- *Will not smother the other person.*
- *Will not bully or be abusive.*

Below, identify some of the ways you have either NOT set boundaries and your partner has taken advantage of you, or you have crossed over the boundaries set by you and your partner.

My/Our Boundaries or Boundaries Not Set	How the Boundary Was Crossed	The End Result

Boundaries are to protect life, not to limit pleasures.
~ Edwin Louis Cole

From your own experiences, what does the above quote mean to you? _____

_____

_____

Setting Boundaries

People addicted to love often do not set boundaries in their relationships. Boundaries can be set for your personal space, sexuality, emotions, thoughts, possessions, time, religion, etc. Below are some of the steps to take in setting boundaries in your current or next relationship.

Be assertive and speak in a clear and non-negotiable manner. Assertive people use "I statements" when speaking to their partners. Based on one of your past relationships, describe your thoughts below:

I feel _____ when you _____ because _____

_____

What I need is _____

_____

Learn to say "no" when you don't want to do something. You can say no without an explanation and without feeling guilty. *What is something to which you should have said "no"?*

_____

_____

_____

_____

Safeguard your space. Set boundaries for your possessions, physical and emotional spaces, and your time and energy. *What is something you didn't set a boundary for that you wish you had?*

_____

_____

_____

_____

Use your support network. If you have doubts or want to run your thoughts about boundaries past other people, rely on your support network. *Who are the positive, supportive, trusted people in your support network?*

_____

_____

_____

_____

Unrealistic Expectations

People who are addicted to love often enter into relationships with unrealistic expectations that no one can meet. Because they often cannot meet their own needs, they have unrealistic expectations that their partner will meet all their needs: financially and emotionally as well as filling their inner void, building self-esteem, etc. *In the hexagons below, identify some of your unrealistic expectations in your current or most recent relationship.*

My Unrealistic Expectations

Unhealthy Relationships

People who are addicted to love often find themselves in unhealthy relationships. Without realizing it ahead of time, or thinking they can make it better, they can become attached to people who are emotionally unavailable, distant, unreceptive, negative, aggressive, dismissive, and/or narcissistic.

Below, explore some of your unhealthy relationships over the years, how you were treated, how long you stayed together, and the relationship outcome.

My Unhealthy Relationships (USE NAME CODES)	How This Person Treated Me	How Long Did It Last and What Was the Relationship Outcome
KAN	KAN constantly belittled me and pressured me to change who I was.	After 3 years, I realized that this person did not care about who I actually am. I left.

Obsessive Behavior

Codependent people often become obsessed and preoccupied with their partner. They feel as if their world revolves around their partner and they give up a great deal of themselves, their interests, and their friends and family. What have you given up?

In each of the four blocks, write about, draw, or doodle what you have given up in your life for someone else. At the bottom explain your wish to have it back or how you can get it back.

An Activity I Gave Up	An Activity I Gave Up
Do I want to get it back? _____ How can I get it back? _____	Do I want to get it back? _____ How can I get it back? _____
An Activity I Gave Up	**An Activity I Gave Up**
Do I want to get it back? _____ How can I get it back? _____	Do I want to get it back? _____ How can I get it back? _____

Fear of Abandonment

Many people grow up with fears of abandonment, and can struggle with "autophobia," an overwhelming fear of being alone or isolated, in which they perceive themselves as being ignored or uncared for, even when they're with another person.

Often, people do not realize they have a fear of abandonment. Complete the table below. Be honest.

Ways People Show a Fear of Abandonment	Ways I Show Fear of Abandonment
Example: Attach quickly, even to unavailable partners or relationships.	*When I meet some people, I automatically begin to think, "This is someone I could be friends with, or a partner with, forever!"*
Attach Quickly, Even to Unavailable Partners or Relationships	
Fail to Commit Fully	
Experience Intense Feelings of Separation Anxiety	
Have Had Very Few Long-Term Relationships	
Move on Quickly Just to Ensure That They Don't Get Too Attached	
Do Everything in Their Power to Please Someone	
Engage In Self-Blame Frequently	
Stay In Relationships No Matter How Unhealthy the Relationship Is	
Feel Insecure and Unworthy Of Love	
Remain Hypersensitive to Criticism	

My Relationships Consume Me

Codependent people who have an addiction to love will be consumed quickly in a relationship. They tend to smother their partners because they are filled with love and romance. They need to be in contact with them several times a day no matter how busy they are.

What are some of the ways you become consumed and fixated on your partner?
Below, identify some of the ways you maintain constant interaction with your partner.

Interaction with My Partner	How I Stay in Contact With My Partner (USE NAME CODE)	How It Affects My Partner (USE NAME CODE)
Email	*I email OLS several times a day at work just to say I Love You!*	*OLS becomes frustrated because she thinks there may be a problem and feels she must check her email to see if there is anything urgent.*
Email		
Text		
Cell Phone Calls		
Social Media		
Face-timing		
Video-Chatting		
Face-to-Face		
Other		
Other		

Are You a People Pleaser?

What is a People Pleaser? It is someone who feels the need to please people, whether they want to or not, for the sake of someone else's feelings or reactions.

See the traits of a people pleaser in the left column. If you think it pertains to you, give an example in the middle column. In the right column, write how else you could have behaved.

A People Pleaser Trait	A Time I Was a People Pleaser	What I Could Have Done Instead
I feel responsible for how someone else feels.		
I constantly apologize.		
I always do what someone wants.		
I can't say NO.		
I do anything to avoid a conflict.		
I feel terrible if anyone is angry at me.		
I pretend to agree when I don't.		
I don't speak up when my feelings are hurt.		
I need praise and compliments to feel good.		
I act like people around me.		

Ways to stop being a people pleaser:
- Ask yourself, "What is most important to me?"
- Determine if people are trying to take advantage of you. It's important to watch out for manipulators and flatterers who just want you to do what they want.
- Asserting yourself when needed.
- Don't feel like you must provide excuses.
- Don't apologize—if it is not your fault.
- Set boundaries and stick to them!

Staying in a Relationship

Codependents will stay in a relationship even though their needs are not being met. They do everything they can, even if they know they shouldn't, to try to keep their partner happy.

Below, journal your thoughts as they relate to you and your relationships.

Have you ever tried to talk yourself into loving someone you weren't particularly fond of simply because you needed the relationship at that time? Explain.

_____

_____

_____

_____

_____

Have you ever felt the need to do a total makeover on your partner early on in your relationship rather than admit that the person wasn't right for you, and you should probably end the relationship? Explain.

_____

_____

_____

_____

_____

When you are in a committed relationship, do you wonder if you chose the right person or fantasize about someone else from your past, thinking you would have been happier with that person? Explain.

_____

_____

_____

_____

_____

Care-Taking

People who are codependent usually want to help other people to the point that they give up their own self-care. Although it is natural to feel empathy and help others, they often put their partner ahead of themselves. They feel the need to help and sometimes feel rejected if the person doesn't want help. They continue to try to help and "fix" the other person. This behavior can become extremely irritating to the other person.

In the rounded squares below, list the ways you want to take care of your partner. Next to the rounded squares below, list the ways you can take care of yourself.

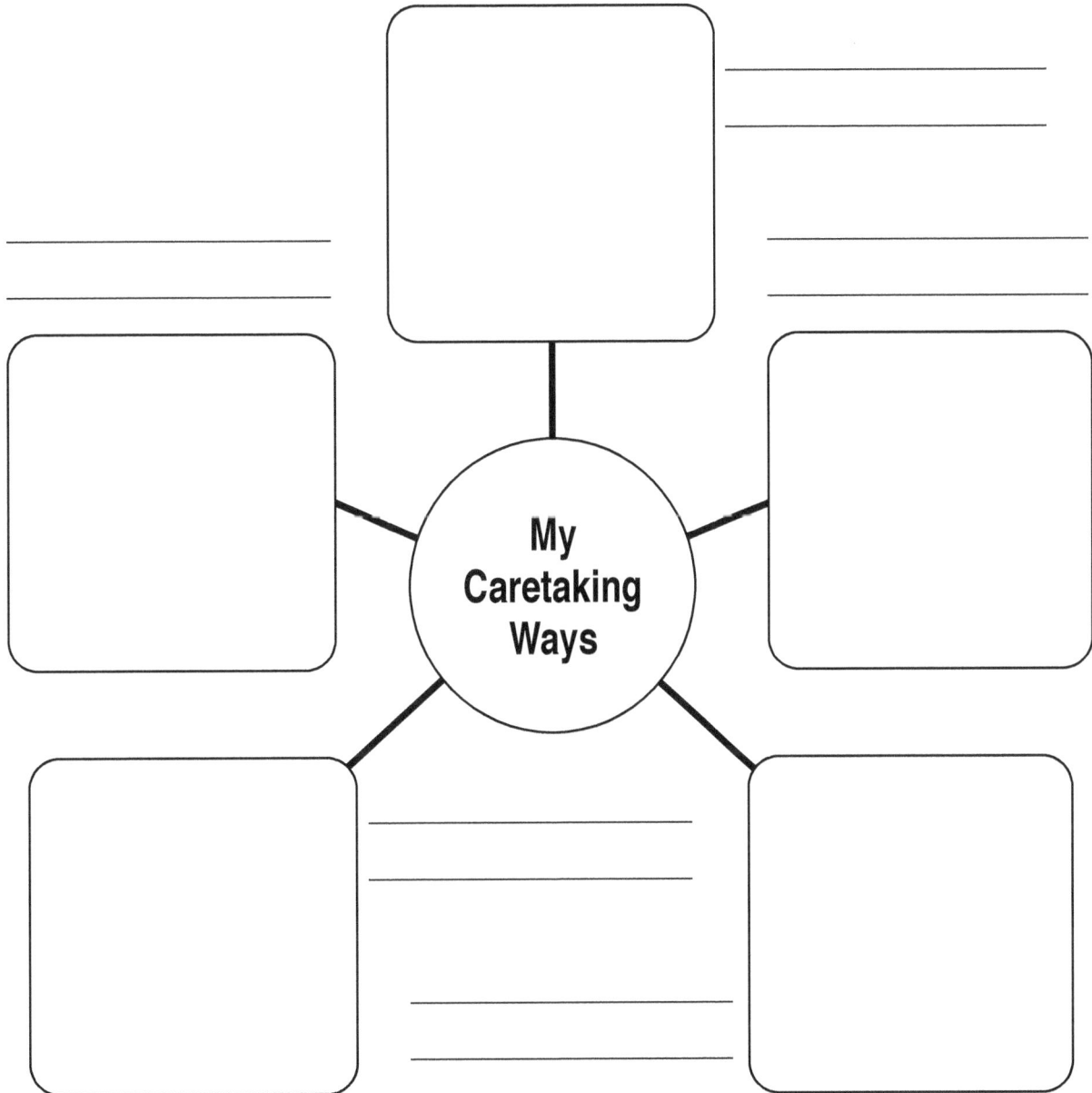

My
Caretaking
Ways

Do you take care of yourself as well as you take care of your partner?

What is Autophobia?

Autophobia: The fear of being alone.
Many people who are addicted to love simply are afraid to be alone.

On the line under each characteristic of autophobia, place an X on the continuum of how much you relate to it. On the dotted line below each one, write why you rated yourself that way. Be HONEST!

I need to control the person in my relationship.

0 (Not Much)　　　　5 (Somewhat)　　　　10 (Very Much)

I complain a lot about the person in my relationships.

0 (Not Much)　　　　5 (Somewhat)　　　　10 (Very Much)

I try to fix the person in my relationship.

0 (Not Much)　　　　5 (Somewhat)　　　　10 (Very Much)

I will smother the person in my relationship.

0 (Not Much)　　　　5 (Somewhat)　　　　10 (Very Much)

I don't communicate my feelings well to the person in my relationship.

0 (Not Much)　　　　5 (Somewhat)　　　　10 (Very Much)

I have problems being intimate with the person in my relationship.

0 (Not Much)　　　　5 (Somewhat)　　　　10 (Very Much)

HIGHER SCORES (Very Much) on each statement indicates that you are experiencing signs of autophobia. You need to be sure that this fear is not prompting an addiction to love.

MEDIUM SCORES (Somewhat) indicate that you are experiencing some signs of autophobia.

LOWER SCORES (Not Much) indicate that you are not experiencing many signs of autophobia.

When It's Over

People who have a relationship addiction often discover that when a relationship ends or a breakup occurs, they experience painful withdrawal symptoms like a withdrawal from a substance abuse. They may feel an extreme sense of betrayal, anger, and pain. They often avoid taking any responsibility and completely blame their partner for not fulfilling unrealistic expectations and relational fantasies.

In the circles below, describe your experiences of some relationships when they were over.

When It's Over

Characteristics of Being Codependent

People who are codependent typically demonstrate several characteristics when in relationships. They often go out of their way to remain in a relationship for fear of abandonment and being alone.

Place a check mark in front of each statement that applies to you and describe why you believe it applies to you.

☐ I tend to love people that feel bad for me, or pity me, and then rescue me.

_____

_____

☐ I feel responsible for the actions of others.

_____

_____

☐ I do more than my share in a relationship to keep the peace.

_____

_____

☐ I am afraid of being abandoned or alone.

_____

_____

☐ I feel responsible for my partner's happiness.

_____

_____

☐ I need approval from my partner.

_____

_____

☐ I am reluctant to trust others.

_____

_____

☐ My moods are controlled by the thoughts and feelings of those around me.

_____

_____

After completing this page, do you believe that you are codependent? _____

If so, are you willing to do work on not being so codependent? _____

Me, In a Relationship ...

People who are addicted to love walk a fine line between wanting to be in relationships for fear of being alone and wanting the buzz they get from being in a new relationship.

Journal your thoughts below.

When I say no to others, I ...

_____

_____

_____

I become emotional in a relationship when ...

_____

_____

_____

I feel compelled to take care of people because ...

_____

_____

_____

If I'm not completely in control, I ...

_____

_____

_____

I smother my romantic partners because ...

_____

_____

_____

When I feel as if I am not liked by everyone, I ...

_____

_____

_____

When I am not in a romantic relationship, I ...

_____

_____

_____

How Important is Independence?

Typically, people who experience codependency find it difficult to spend time alone or do anything alone. To overcome a codependent personality, it is important to become more independent. You can start by doing things by yourself without feeling like you always need to be with someone. Independent people have no problem going out to dinner alone, going to the movies alone, starting a new hobby, or joining a new class.

Discuss with your group members or mental health professional how you can spend time alone. Write about them, draw them, or doodle them in the boxes below.

Codependent people have grown to be dependent on others for self-fulfillment. People can learn to be content being alone rather than fearing being alone.

Healing from codependency means one needs to face one's fear of loneliness.

Quotes about Codependency

Read all three of the quotations below.

#1

There are almost as many definitions of codependency
as there are experiences that represent it.
~ Melody Beattie

#2

Loss of a relationship is painful, but if you lose yourself in
a relationship, when it ends, it's devastating, because you are lost.
~ Darlene Lancer

#3

Relationships are the hallmark of the mature person.
~ Brian Tracy

Pick a quote that sounds like you and explain why. #_____

_____

_____

_____

Pick one that inspires you to do better and explain how you will do that. # _____

_____

_____

_____

Pick a quote that taught you something and explain what it taught you. # _____

_____

_____

_____

Write your very own quote regarding relationships and what you have learned.

_____

_____

_____

Love Addiction Costs

Name _____

Date _____

Love Addiction Costs Assessment
Introduction and Directions

Healthy romantic love can be a beautiful experience. Unfortunately, addictive love is a different type of love and is often far from a beautiful experience. When individuals are preoccupied with falling and being in love, they tend to engage in many highly regrettable behaviors to the point of obsession.

This assessment contains 20 statements related to the problems of someone addicted to the buzz of new love relationships. Read each of the statements and decide whether or not it describes you. Circle the number next to that item under the TRUE column if it is TRUE. If the statement is FALSE, circle the number next to that item under the FALSE column.

In the following example, the circled number 2 under TRUE indicates the statement is true of the person completing the inventory:

As a result of desperately needing someone to love ...	TRUE	FALSE
I become sad very easily	(2)	1
I constantly experience anxiety	2	1

This is not a test. Since there are no right or wrong answers, do not spend too much time thinking about your answers. Be sure to respond to every statement.

BE HONEST!

If you choose, no one else needs to see the results.

(Turn to the next page and begin.)

Love Addiction Costs Assessment

Name _____ Date _____

This will only be accurate if you respond honestly. No one else needs to see this if you choose.

As a result of desperately needing someone to love ...	TRUE	FALSE
I become sad very easily	2	1
I constantly experience anxiety	2	1
I have legal problems	2	1
I don't feel good about myself anymore	2	1
I have ruined many relationships	2	1
I have trouble at work or school	2	1
I am an emotional wreck	2	1
I have financial difficulties	2	1
I have lost interest in spending time with family members	2	1
I am neglecting my friends	2	1
I no longer engage in my hobbies, classes, meetings, etc.	2	1
I notice that the things that I used to like no longer hold my interest	2	1
I have obsessive thoughts about potential partners	2	1
I have stalked people I want to meet	2	1
I have had many breakups or divorces	2	1
I am considered a "serial dater"	2	1
I could have advanced in my career more if I wasn't so obsessed	2	1
I have or have had a sexually transmitted disease	2	1
I have experienced abuse	2	1
I use substances to cope	2	1

Love Addiction Costs TOTAL = _____

Go to the next page for scoring assessment
results, profile interpretation, and individual descriptions

Love Addiction Costs Assessment

Scoring Directions

People who are addicted to love demonstrate an unusual pattern in which they become addicted to the feeling of being in a new, exciting romantic relationship. They often become *serial daters* and continue searching for the *perfect partner,* or once they are in a committed relationship, they become co-dependent and smother their partners. This obsession causes many problems!

The assessment you just completed is designed to help you explore your level of addiction to love and the problems related to searching for the *perfect* partner. **On the previous page, total the scores you circled and transfer that number below. Then place that number on the continuum line of the matching scale below to find your level of love addiction.**

Perfection is achieved, not when there is nothing more to add,
but when there is nothing left to take away.
~ Antoine de Saint-Exupery

Assessment Profile Interpretation

Place your score below and then profile it by placing an X on the continuum that follows. The higher your score, the greater your addiction is.

Love Addiction Score = _____

20 = Low	30 = Moderate	40 = High

How can you stop expecting perfectionistic traits of your romantic partner and your romantic relationship?

_____

_____

_____

Share your responses with your mental health professional or others in your group.

Financial Consequences

One of the primary consequences for people who have a love issue is the loss of financial resources. They typically do this to avoid being alone (if not in a relationship) or abandoned (if in a relationship). There are several ways these two scenarios can occur.

Complete the following table with your own experiences.

Financial Consequences	Not in a relationship	In a Relationship (USE NAME CODE)	How I Mismanaged my Finances
Example: Giving too much money		*MPG I thought my partner just liked to go to the casino for dinner and play the slots. She said she'd only invest $20 and then go.*	*I gave my partner a great deal of money when she had gambling debts. I was afraid she would leave me if I didn't.*
Example: Giving too much money	*I gave a cute guy who had a sign up on the street, "need food money," a lot of money each week and asked him to go out.*		*I found out that he lived in a nice house with a family and didn't like to work, so this is how he made money.*
Giving Too Much Money			
Helping My Partner			
Paying Bills for My Partner			
Buying Gifts			
Spending More Than Necessary			
Going Places to Search for the Perfect Partner			
Other			

How can you manage your finances better by feeling you do not NEED to be in a relationship?

_____

_____

_____

© 2023 WHOLE PERSON ASSOCIATES, 101 WEST 2ND STREET, SUITE 203, DULUTH MN 55802 • 800-247-6789 • WHOLEPERSON.COM

My Other Addictions

People addicted to love often become addicted to other things besides their relationship: food, exercise, gambling, gaming, sex, shopping, substances, technology, or work. They will have another addiction to escape from the despair and unhappiness within an addictive relationship. Some will have another addiction if they have lost a relationship, are in withdrawal, are lonely, or are in-between a relationship.

Below, identify how you use other addictions.

My Other Addictions	How I Use These Addictions	Other Ways I Could Cope
Food	When I am anxious or upset, I just keep eating to the point of feeling bloated and sick afterward.	I could take a walk outside and notice the beauty of nature, even if it's a little busy and on the sidewalk.
Food		
Exercise		
Gambling		
Gaming		
Sex		
Shopping		
Substances		
Technology		
Work		
Other		

There are all kinds of addicts, I guess. We all have pain.
And we all look for ways to make the pain go away.
~ Sherman Alexi

What is your preferred method for making the pain go away?_____

Physical Symptoms of Withdrawal

The consequences of addictive loving are at their very worst when a relationship ends. Since a love addict's relationship is the essential aspect of their life as their identity is usually wrapped up in the relationship, the person is often sad and disoriented when it ends. Physical withdrawal symptoms typically occur when reality seeps in.

Below are some physical symptoms of withdrawal from a relationship. Place a checkmark in the front box of those that apply to you and describe how you are affected.

☐ Anxiety _____

_____

☐ Dizzy _____

_____

☐ Fever and chills _____

_____

☐ Flu-like symptoms _____

_____

☐ Insomnia _____

_____

☐ Nausea _____

_____

☐ Sweating _____

_____

☐ Tension _____

_____

☐ Tingling _____

_____

☐ Vomiting _____

_____

☐ Weight-loss _____

_____

Emotional Symptoms of Withdrawal

The consequences of addictive loving are at their worst when a relationship ends. Since the love addict's relationship is the essential aspect of their life and their identity is usually wrapped up in the relationship, it often leaves the person disoriented and devastated when it ends. Emotional withdrawal symptoms typically occur when reality seeps in.

Below are some emotional symptoms of withdrawal from a relationship. Place a checkmark in the front box of those that apply to you and describe how you are affected.

☐ Agitation _____

_____

☐ Depression _____

_____

☐ Distorted and irrational thinking _____

_____

☐ Fearful and worried thoughts _____

_____

☐ Numbness _____

_____

☐ Out of control and powerless _____

_____

☐ Over-reactions _____

_____

☐ Mood changes _____

_____

☐ Panic _____

_____

☐ Sleep and dream or nightmare issues _____

_____

☐ Stress _____

_____

Dangerous Romances

People with an addiction to love often find themselves involved in a dangerous romance with a toxic partner who uses sexual activity to hold on to a relationship or uses sexuality to attract potential partners. Have you ever been involved in a dangerous relationship?

Journal about your dangerous relationships below.

Dangerous Situation #1

What occurred?_____

_____

How were you in danger?_____

_____

Were others in danger?_____

_____

How did you handle the situation?_____

_____

How could you have handled the situation in a better way, or are you satisfied with the way you handled it?

_____

_____

Dangerous Situation #2

What occurred?_____

_____

How were you in danger?_____

_____

Were others in danger?_____

_____

How did you handle the situation?_____

_____

How could you have handled the situation in a better way, or are you satisfied with the way you handled it?

_____

_____

Self-Destructive Behavior

People with a love addiction often develop self-destructive behavior as a coping mechanism, such as self-mutilation, cutting, alcohol abuse, drug abuse, compulsive overeating, excessive spending, etc.

Below, write, draw, or doodle your self-destructive behaviors.

The effects of unresolved trauma can be devastating. It can affect our habits and outlook on life, leading to addictions and poor decision-making. It can take a toll on our family life and interpersonal relationships. It can trigger real physical pain, symptoms, and disease. And it can lead to a range of self-destructive behaviors.

~ Peter A. Levine

Is there an unresolved trauma in your background? How can you resolve your feelings about it? Who is someone you can trust that can help? (USE NAME CODE)

_____

_____

_____

Legal Problems

Addictive love can lead to trouble with the law. Some behaviors carried out by lovers that violate the law may include harassment, damage to property, sexual or physical abuse, prostitution, drugs, stealing, or other illegal activities. These behaviors can lead to arrest and incarceration, loss of career mobility, lawsuits, or other legal consequences.

In the squares below, identify any legal problem you have experienced due to your addiction to love, and describe the outcome of these legal problems.

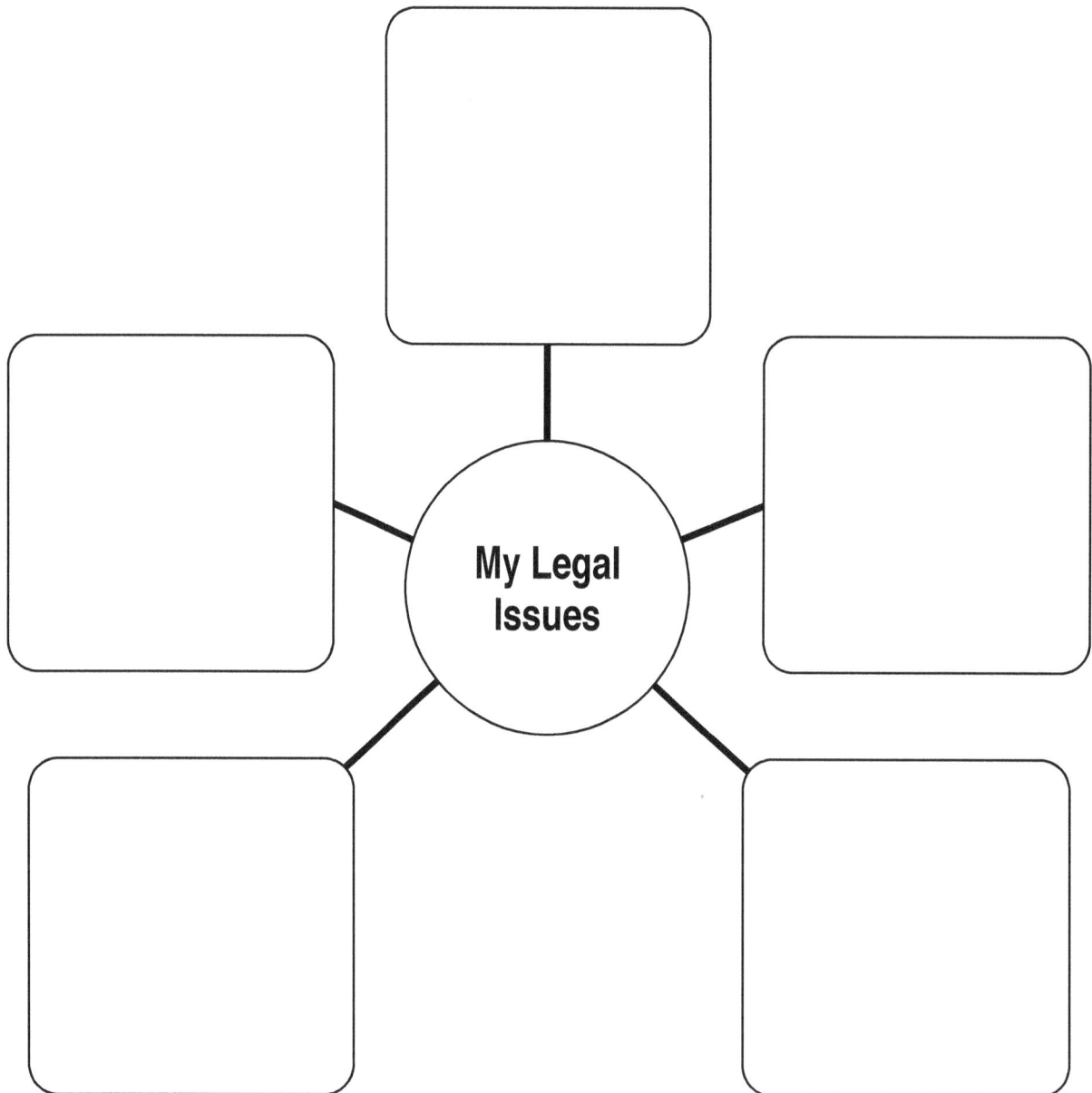

My Legal Issues

Guilt and Shame

People addicted to love have many behaviors for which they feel guilt or shame. Below, write about how you have felt guilty and how you have felt ashamed of your choice of relationships or your addiction to love.

I feel guilty about _____

_____

_____

    I can resolve this and forgive myself by _____

_____

_____

I feel guilty about _____

_____

_____

    I can resolve this and forgive myself by _____

_____

_____

I am ashamed of _____

_____

_____

    I can resolve this and forgive myself by _____

_____

_____

I am ashamed of _____

_____

_____

    I can resolve this and forgive myself by _____

_____

_____

Relationship Problems

One would surmise that people addicted to love would have great relationships. However, quite the opposite is often true. The person addicted to love can have problems that usually occur in the relationships that they are involved in, whether it be with their partner, children, parents, family, or because of divorce, breakups, parenting issues, lack of friends, finances, jealousy, boundaries, emotions, sexual intimacy, selfishness, faithfulness, etc.

In each section below, list the problems that you are experiencing. (USE NAME CODES)

Relationship	Problems I Experience in this Relationship
Parents	
Partner or Spouse	
Children	
Family Members	
Friends	
People in the Community	
Co-workers or boss	
Other	

Job Performance Issues

People dealing with an addiction to love often experience difficulties at work related to their job performance. They are often so preoccupied and obsessed with their present relationship that they are unable to continue to perform well at their jobs.

Below, place a check mark in front of the problematic work issues that describe you. In the space by each warning sign you have checked, explain how it pertains to you.

Problematic Issues at Work

☐ Job Loss _____
_____
_____

☐ Performance _____
_____
_____

☐ Reliability _____
_____
_____

☐ Harassment _____
_____
_____

☐ Gossip _____
_____
_____

☐ Late for Work _____
_____
_____

☐ Work Absence_____
_____
_____

☐ Phone calls or texts _____
_____
_____

☐ Failing to Finish Projects _____
_____
_____

☐ Other _____
_____
_____

☐ Other _____
_____
_____

Hurting Myself

Not being in a relationship, feeling lonely, alone, or abandoned can cause sadness and frustration for people addicted to love. They can find that when they are without a partner for extended periods, they may be tempted to hurt themselves by slashing, burning, scratching, piercing skin, pulling hair, cutting, hitting themselves, and even thinking about suicide.

How have you hurt yourself, or thought about hurting yourself, due to your need to have a love relationship? Below, list those times, what you did, and how you could have dealt with your pain in a safe way.

How I Have Felt about Not Having a Partner	How I Tried to Hurt Myself	Other Ways I Can Cope
Example: I feel hopeless about finding the perfect person.	I harm myself in places I can cover up with my clothing.	I could talk to a trusted person in my support network when I feel the urge to hurt myself.

My Suicidal Thoughts and/or Attempts	What Made Me Stop	How I Can Avoid These Thoughts
Example: As my feelings of hopelessness increase, I get sadder and don't care whether I live or not.	A person in my support group reminded me that I do not need another person to be whole. I am good enough!	Every time I get sad and start to feel hopeless, I can remember to use positive affirmations to feel better. I need to go regularly to someone I trust to talk!

Ways to deal with your feelings and desires to hurt yourself:
- Remember, you are not alone.
- Find healthy alternatives to hurting yourself.
- Be open and talk with trusted family and friends.
- Seek help from your mental health therapist, doctor, or other health provider.
- Create your own support system. Have a paper with names, email, phones, etc.
- **Call the National Suicide Prevention Lifeline in the U.S. at 1-800-273-8255.**

Hurting Others

People who are addicted to love and are not in a romantic relationship will often hurt themselves when they are alone. They may also be prone to hurt others who reject them or abandon them in a relationship. This retaliation can often include violent behavior to a betrayed spouse or partner, sexual partner, family member, or a significant other of a romantic partner.

Explore the times you have tried or thought about hurting others and the outcome.

Unacceptable Ways to Hurt Others, Either Physically or Emotionally	My Experiences	Outcome Of My Behavior Or My Partner's Behavior
Stalking		
Domestic Violence		
Emotional Abuse		
Cyberstalking		
Posting Damaging Photos or Information Online		
Attempted Homicide		
Other		

Ways to deal with your feelings and desire to hurt others:
- Talk to a medical professional.
- Talk with people in your support system.
- Find healthy alternatives for dealing with your anger.
- Take time out to think before you act.
- Take deep breaths or take a walk.
- Meditate before acting.

Values and Beliefs

All relationships require some compromise. Partners often find themselves in relationships in which there are major conflicts arising from the differences in each one's spiritual beliefs, personal needs, values, etc. They may feel that they are being asked to give up who they are!

Examples of these might include not being able to go to their own house of worship; the inability to further their education; being unable to be with their friends and family; unable to eat the foods they particularly like, etc.

Think about some of the values and beliefs which you have compromised or given up to accommodate a relationship. Describe them and how you and your partner could have compromised.

Belief or Value Asked to Give Up		Compromise to Make
Example: Going to my house of worship	⇨	I will go to my house of worship and you can stay home or come with me and I will go with you to yours next week.
Example: Going to my friend's family gathering	⇨	My partner doesn't value friendship or family. I will go alone to the gathering.
	⇨	
	⇨	
	⇨	
	⇨	
	⇨	
	⇨	

All compromise is based on give and take, but there can be no give and take
on fundamentals. Any compromise on mere fundamentals is a surrender.
For it is all give and no take.
~ Mahatma Gandhi

Coping by Expressing Emotions

People who are addicted to love and relationships experience a wide variety of emotions which they hold inside and do not express to their partner or anyone else. They don't express them to their partner for fear of being alone again, or because they are afraid of not being able to meet anyone else.

They don't share them with a trusted person for fear that they will get advice they don't want to hear. When one holds in these emotions, it can have a negative impact on the person's emotional and mental health.

It is extremely important and healthy to cope with these emotions by sharing them with one's partner, or if that is not an option, with a trusted, supportive person.

Below, identify your emotions, when you tend to experience them, and with whom you share them.

Emotions	When I Have These Emotions	How I Usually Cope with These Emotions By Sharing Them with…
Example: Anger	*My partner doesn't express his love for me. If I say "I love you" he says "good."*	*I ask him why and he says he shouldn't need to tell me. I told my sister and she said I should "dump" him. I don't want to be alone.*
Anger		
Anxiety		
Defensiveness		
Embarrassment		
Fear		
Guilt		
Hopelessness		
Sadness		
Other		

Try these ways to cope with your emotions rather than holding them in:
- Take a few deep breaths in and let them out. This can help to calm your mind and lower your blood pressure.
- Let go of negative energy with a vigorous spin class, practicing Tai Chi, or taking a run through the park.
- Welcome positive energy into your life by dancing to your favorite song.
- Journal to process your negative thoughts. By taking a few minutes each day to write down your thoughts, you can start to work through your difficult feelings, and take ownership of your response.

Unrealistic Views

People with an addiction to love usually have unrealistic views of effective relationships. They live in a constant state of fantasy where everything is absolutely perfect in a relationship.

Identify your current unrealistic views of relationships, and BELOW, identify more realistic views of relationships.

Current Unrealistic Views of Relationships

What I am Learning About Realistic Relationships

What is the first thing you can do to take on a more realistic view of any relationship?

_____

_____

_____

© 2023 WHOLE PERSON ASSOCIATES, 101 WEST 2ND STREET, SUITE 203, DULUTH MN 55802 • 800-247-6789 • WHOLEPERSON.COM

Quotes About the Cost of a Love Addiction

Read all three of the quotations below.

#1

Personal relationships are the fertile soil from which all advancement,
all success, all achievement in real life grows.
~ Ben Stein

#2

Every day we have plenty of opportunities to get angry, stressed or
offended. But what you're doing when you indulge these negative emotions
is giving something outside yourself power over your happiness.
You can choose to not let little things upset you.
~ Joel Osteen

#3

The worst guilt is to accept an unearned guilt.
~ Ayn Rand

Pick a quote that sounds like you and explain why. #_____

_____

_____

_____

Pick one that inspires you to do better and explain how you will do that. # _____

_____

_____

_____

Pick a quote that taught you something and explain what it taught you. # _____

_____

_____

_____

Write your very own quote regarding relationships and what you have learned.

_____

_____

_____

Love Yourself

Name _____

Date _____

Love Yourself Assessment
Introduction and Directions

People who are addicted to love are so busy trying to find the perfect partner or trying to stay in a relationship for fear of being alone, that they do not take the time to really love themselves. To truly overcome an addiction of love, they must learn to understand and love who they truly are.

It will be helpful to explore how much you love yourself to truly understand why you feel the need to be in a relationship in order to feel whole and complete.

The following assessment contains 15 statements that will help you explore your current level of self-love. Read each of the statements and decide if the statement describes you. If it does, circle the number under the YES column. If the statement does not describe you, circle the number under the NO column.

In the following example, the circled 2 indicates that the statement describes the person completing this assessment:

When it comes to loving myself...   YES   NO

I am aware of my gifts and talents, and I use them . . . . (2) 1

I praise myself daily. 2 1

This is not a test. Since there are no right or wrong answers, do not spend too much time thinking about your answers. Be sure to respond to every statement.

BE HONEST!

If you choose, no one else needs to see the results.

(Turn to the next page and begin.)

Love Yourself Assessment

Name _____ Date _____

This will only be accurate if you respond honestly. No one else needs to see this if you choose.

When it comes to loving myself...   YES   NO

I am aware of my gifts and talents, and I use them 2 1

I praise myself daily 2 1

I am extremely self-critical 1 2

I challenge myself 2 1

My self-worth is based on how people feel about me 1 2

I will do anything to avoid a partner disagreeing with me 1 2

I define my own worth and lovability 2 1

I When I look in the mirror I do not like who I see 1 2

I feel guilty if I take time for myself 1 2

When in a social situation, I can relax and be myself 2 1

When I make a mistake, I forgive myself and learn 2 1

I look for ways to improve my self-confidence 2 1

I give others a break, but I don't give myself one 1 2

I can have fun all by myself 2 1

I compare myself to others and become depressed 1 2

TOTAL Answers = _____

Go to the next page for scoring assessment
results, profile interpretation, and individual descriptions

Love Yourself Assessment

Scoring and Profile Interpretations

The assessment you just completed is designed to measure how much you love yourself. Count the numbers you circled on the Love Yourself Assessment. Put that total on the line marked TOTAL on the assessment at the bottom of the page. Then, transfer your total to this space below:

TOTAL = _____

Assessment Profile Interpretation

By circling even ONE number one response, you should think about the importance of loving yourself. The more number one responses you circled, the greater the risk you have for experiencing difficult relationship issues because of your lack of confidence and lack of self-love.

The LOWER your score on the Love Yourself Assessment, the more of a lack of love for yourself you are experiencing.

15 = Low	**22 = Moderate**	**30 = High**

How honest were you when completing the assessment? Is your score valid?

_____

_____

What is your reaction to your score?

_____

_____

What actions do you need to take to love yourself more? Why do you think so?

_____

_____

Don't Wait for Others! Compliment Yourself!

Give yourself some compliments! Write your compliments in the categories below. Compliment yourself for your accomplishments.

Example: I made a great chocolate cake and I brought it to the fire station where my partner works.

1. _____

2. _____

3. _____

4. _____

5. _____

Compliment yourself for your personal characteristics:

Example: I made a smooth presentation at work last week. I am a great communicator.

1. _____

2. _____

3. _____

4. _____

5. _____

Compliment yourself for kind things you have done for someone else lately:

Example: I offered to baby sit with my partner's granddaughter.

1. _____

2. _____

3. _____

4. _____

5. _____

It's Time to Love Yourself!

Love addicts usually do not love themselves. Instead, they expect to receive love from others. They are constantly searching for people to tell them how worthy they are, how capable they are, and how lovable they are. Now, it is time to love yourself!

List the things you love about yourself. *Example: I love that I am a supportive friend, I love my hair, I love my sense of humor, I love my work ethic, I love my outgoing personality.*

I love _____

_____

I love _____

_____

I love _____

_____

I love _____

_____

I love _____

_____

I love _____

_____

I love _____

_____

I love _____

_____

Love yourself first and everything else falls into line. You really have to love yourself to get anything done in this world.
~ Lucille Ball

Do Not Expect Relationships to Complete You

An important aspect for recovering love addicts is learning skills for healthier relationships in general, as well as healthier love lives. People do not need romantic or sexual relationships to enjoy lives filled with joy. It is important to learn new behaviors that can replace old, unhealthy patterns.

Below, identify some of your old patterns, and then identify new patterns that you will implement to live a more meaningful life. (USE NAME CODES)

Old Patterns	New & Improved Patterns
Example: Neglecting my family members.	Reconnect with my father, mother, and brother.
Example: Not going to a movie I want to see because TKG doesn't want to.	Ask someone else to go or go alone.

Below are potential reasons your relationships with others can break down.
- Trust issues.
- Financial fights.
- Communication breakdowns.
- Constantly fighting and arguing.
- Arguments that get out of control.
- Not feeling understood or being emotioinally distant.

Which one of the above is the main reason your relationships break down? Explain. _____

_____

How can you make sure it doesn't affect your attempts to reconnect with important people in

the future? _____

_____

What is Self-Esteem?

Self-Esteem is a person's overall sense of self-worth or personal value.
It is how much you appreciate and like yourself.

Below, put a ✔ *the box as to define how each sign describes you. On the lines, write why you responded that way.*

Signs of Good Self-Esteem:

☐ Confidence in myself.

_____

_____

☐ Ability to say no to others.

_____

_____

☐ Positive outlook on life and relationships.

_____

_____

☐ Awareness of my overall strengths and weaknesses and acceptance of them.

_____

_____

☐ Negative experiences do not taint my overall life perspective.

_____

_____

☐ Ability to express my needs to others.

_____

_____

You may not control all the events that happen to you,
but you can decide not to be reduced by them.
~ Maya Angelou

How can you maintain your self-esteem? _____

_____

_____

Positive Affirmations

Positive affirmations are short phrases or mantras that you repeat to yourself. They describe a specific outcome you desire or who you want to be. At first, these affirmations might not be true, but with constant repetition, you will start to believe them. You will find that eventually, these affirmations will become your reality.

Below are the steps in developing affirmations. For each step, begin developing an affirmation you can say to yourself daily.

1. Affirmations start with the words "I am…"
2. Affirmations need to be positive. Avoid using the words not or never or should or could.
3. Affirmations are short and specifically related to you.
4. Affirmations are made in the present tense.
5. Affirmations are about yourself. They are about your own behavior, not someone else's.

Examples:
"I am a worthwhile person."
"I love myself whether I am in a relationship or not."
"My greatest love is the love of myself."

Now you write your own. In the six boxes below, create some positive affirmations about your love for yourself. Then cut them out and place them in prominent places where you will see them and can repeat them each day, until they come to you automatically. On the line under the affirmation write where you will post them.

Where did you decide to post your affirmation? _____

Bathroom mirror? Car? On the refrigerator? On your computer?_____

You can transfer them to a sticky note. _____

Forgive Yourself

People who are in unhealthy relationships, or who are constantly chasing the perfect love partner to make themselves whole, usually have a problem forgiving themselves for mistakes they have made, or mistakes they think they have made in the past. They dwell on them! Everyone makes poor choices from time to time. By reflecting on one's mistakes, a person can learn to forgive oneself, pledge to do better, and then move on! Loving yourself unconditionally despite any mistakes you made in the past is important for self-esteem and personal growth.

Below, describe some mistakes you have made and how you can forgive yourself.

Mistakes I Have Made	How I Dwell on Them	How I Can Forgive Myself and Move on.
Example: I was so intent on finding the perfect relationship that I neglected my career.	I became envious of my co-workers who were being promoted. I was rude to them, and it wasn't their fault.	I can start focusing on work, take a few classes, and get a promotion too.

Anyone who has never made a mistake has never tried anything new.
~ Albert Einstein

Love Yourself by Saying "No" to Others

Sometimes we do way too much for people because we like to please them. We tend to stretch ourselves too thin and commit to everything asked of us. This is especially true for people who are addicted to love. They feel they need a romantic relationship so much that they forget to look after themselves and say "no" to some requests.

In the hexagons below, identify the people to whom you cannot say "no." Explain why.

I Can't Say No Too...

With your mental health professional or with the members of your group practice ways you can say "NO".

Pursue New Interests

People addicted to love spend all their free time thinking about relationships, how they can be in a relationship, or how they can feel the buzz of a new romantic relationship. They rarely focus on what they can do for themselves. If this describes you, you need to begin thinking of ways to care about yourself. This is a great time to try something new, perhaps something that you have wanted to try for a while or have been too afraid to do.

You never know what you might enjoy until you try it. Think of a new hobby you could try (writing songs), a way you might improve yourself (learn French) or go to a place you've wanted to go to for a while (visit the museums in your area).

Below, write, draw, or doodle four new interests you would be willing to pursue.

Interest #1	Interest #2
Interest #3	**Interest #4**

Circle the interest you will commit to pursuing within a week.   1   2   3   4

Care for Yourself

In overcoming an addiction to love and relationships, it is important that you take daily actions to enhance your overall well-being and care for yourself. Below are several ways you could be showing your body and mind self-love in your everyday life.

On the line under each critical daily action, place an X on the continuum to indicate how much the statement describes you. On the dotted line below each one, write why you rated yourself that way. Be HONEST!

I sleep at least 8 hours per night.

0 (Not Much)   5 (Somewhat)   10 (Very Much)

I eat healthy meals while limiting junk food and sugary beverages.

0 (Not Much)   5 (Somewhat)   10 (Very Much)

I give myself time and space to practice spirituality, religion, etc.

0 (Not Much)   5 (Somewhat)   10 (Very Much)

I exercise regularly.

0 (Not Much)   5 (Somewhat)   10 (Very Much)

I spend time reflecting and meditating.

0 (Not Much)   5 (Somewhat)   10 (Very Much)

I take time to relax when I need to.

0 (Not Much)   5 (Somewhat)   10 (Very Much)

HIGHER SCORES *(Very Much)* on each statement indicate you are taking daily actions to care for yourself.

MEDIUM SCORES *(Somewhat)* indicate that you are taking some daily actions to care for yourself.

LOWER SCORES *(Not Much)* indicate that you are not taking enough daily actions to care for yourself. Remember that the more you care for yourself, the sooner you can cut the ties that bind you to a love addiction.

© 2023 WHOLE PERSON ASSOCIATES, 101 WEST 2ND STREET, SUITE 203, DULUTH MN 55802 • 800-247-6789 • WHOLEPERSON.COM

What's Your Purpose?

People who love themselves, and do not feel that they need to be in a relationship to be complete, or to have some sort of purpose, will not become addicted to love. You have a unique purpose whether you are in a relationship or not! Understanding what you want and where you want to go is crucial to being happy and finding purpose and meaning in your life.

Respond to the following questions to explore your unique purpose:

What were you passionate about as a child? Can you rekindle this passion?

_____

_____

_____

What kind of work or job would you do even if you did not get paid for it? Find it!

_____

_____

_____

What makes you forget about the world around you? Can you get more involved?

_____

_____

_____

What world issues bother you? What can you do about it?

_____

_____

_____

What types of people do you spend time with and what do you talk about? How can you find more time to do that?

_____

_____

_____

What is on your bucket list to accomplish? Make a plan!

_____

_____

_____

What is your non-relationship-based dream, and how could you make it happen?

_____

_____

_____

Do Things That Make You Feel Good

People addicted to love only feel good when they are in a relationship, or when they are chasing a relationship. Think about ways you can feel good physically, emotionally, creatively, and spiritually, without being in a relationship.

Below, write down some of the activities that make you feel good in each category ... and then ... start doing them!

Methods	What Would Make Me Feel Good?	How I Can Pursue These Activities?
Physically *Example: Begin a new exercise regimen*		
Creatively *Example: Write an article or a book*		
Emotionally *Example: Keep a positivity journal*		
Spiritually *Example: Meditate*		

If you want to feel good, you have to go out and do some good.
~ Oprah Winfrey

© 2023 WHOLE PERSON ASSOCIATES, 101 WEST 2ND STREET, SUITE 203, DULUTH MN 55802 • 800-247-6789 • WHOLEPERSON.COM

Thank Others

People addicted to love focus on the future and not what they currently have. One way to overcome an addiction to love, is to lovingly thank those people currently in your life. In essence, thanking those around you is one of the best ways to love yourself.

In each of the rounded squares, list a person who is in your life and whom you want to thank. Then, write why you are thankful for the person in the space nearby.

People For Whom I Am Thankful

Being grateful can fill a heart. Now, tell these people why you are thankful for them!

Avoiding Vices and Toxic Influences

For love addicts, temptation is everywhere! It is important to explore both your vices and toxic influences. Vices (activities like relying on substances, going to bars, and using your job to meet potential romantic partners) and toxic influences (people who feel you MUST have a romantic partner) will keep you dependent on others and prevent you from loving yourself.

Complete the tables below to examine your vices and toxic influences.

Vices	How I Use These Vices	How I Will Avoid Them
Example: Using alcohol to cope with my loneliness.	*I use substances to lower my inhibitions and be bolder in meeting potential partners.*	*I will avoid situations where alcohol is served.*

Toxic Influences (USE NAME CODES)	How I Am Influenced	How I Deal with My Toxic Influences
Example: MSS	*She keeps introducing me to new potential partners.*	*Be assertive and tell her that I am concentrating on my career, not romantic relationships.*

Some helpful hints:
- You always have options.
- Set boundaries and limits on high-risk behavior.
- Connect to others with empathy, attention, and respect.
- Do not view people you meet as potential romantic partners.
- Analyze your alternatives or options before deciding what to do.
- Be assertive if you do not want to do something or go somewhere.

Thank You

People who are addicted to love most often love others more than they love themselves. They do not know how to express their love for themselves.

Fill in the spaces that follow about your love of yourself and thank yourself.

I am very thankful to ME for the following reasons:

_____

_____

_____

_____

_____

_____

_____

_____

_____

I am thankful for trying to love myself more and trying to overcome an addiction to love!

_____

_____

_____

_____

_____

_____

_____

_____

_____

Supportive People Who Love Me

In order to love yourself, you need to surround yourself with people who treat you with kindness and respect. The people with whom you spend time reflect how you feel about yourself. People who feel worthy surround themselves with positive, supportive people.

Sometimes loving yourself means you must end a relationship that is unhealthy and hurtful to you.

In each circle, identify the people (USE NAME CODES) *who are positive and support you. In the space next to each name code, write how that person supports you.*

ME

© 2023 WHOLE PERSON ASSOCIATES, 101 WEST 2ND STREET, SUITE 203, DULUTH MN 55802 • 800-247-6789 • WHOLEPERSON.COM

Quotes about Loving Yourself

Read all three of the quotations below.

#1

A failure is not always a mistake, it may simply be the best one can do under the circumstances. The real mistake is to stop trying.
~ B. F. Skinner

#2

You have to be able to love yourself because that's when things fall into place.
~ Vanessa Hudgens

#3

I'm not looking for 'outer esteem' anymore, what they call 'other esteem.' I'm looking for self-esteem. And people think that self-esteem is built with accomplishments. And, 'Hey, look what I did in my life.'
~ Lisa Lampanelli

Pick a quote that sounds like you and explain why. #_____

_____

_____

_____

Pick one that inspires you to do better and explain how you will do that. # _____

_____

_____

_____

Pick a quote that taught you something and explain what it taught you. # _____

_____

_____

_____

Write your very own quote regarding relationships and what you have learned.

_____

_____

_____

WholePerson

Whole Person Associates is the leading publisher of training resources for professionals who empower people to create and maintain healthy lifestyles. Our creative resources will help you work effectively with your clients in the areas of stress management, wellness promotion, mental health, and life skills.

Please visit us at our website: **WholePerson.com**. You can check out our entire line of products, place an order, request our print catalog, and sign up for our monthly special notifications.

Whole Person Associates
800-247-6789
Books@WholePerson.com

www.ingramcontent.com/pod-product-compliance
Lightning Source LLC
Chambersburg PA
CBHW082359270326
41935CB00013B/1685